MENOPAUSE, ADHD AND THE MYTH OF MULTITASKING

The Midlife Plot Twist No One Warned us About

Kelly Haider, MS, LPC

Disclaimer

This book is not intended to substitute for professional medical, psychological, or psychiatric advice, diagnosis, or treatment. Readers should consult with qualified healthcare providers for individualized guidance.

For my husband, Laer —Thank you for loving me through every version of myself, for holding steady when everything else shifted, and for being the only person I'd ever want to survive this hormone season with.

TABLE OF CONTENTS

Introduction

I'm a mental-health therapist — which is why I thought I should have known what was happening to me. I've spent years helping clients understand their brains, their emotions, and their patterns. I just didn't realize I'd need the same compassion and explanation for myself. It's humbling to be the expert and the patient at the same time.

When my heart started racing for no reason and I was sweating all the time — when my focus disappeared and I couldn't follow what the people closest to me were saying — I didn't think, "Ah, hormones." I thought, "Something's really wrong with me." So, I did what people do— I pathologized myself. I thought maybe it was anxiety, or burnout, or a heart condition. I ran every test. I saw every specialist. And every time, the results came back the same: Normal. Except nothing about me felt normal.

I was tested for perimenopause too. But no one said, "Hey, this is what's happening to your body and your brain." No one explained that the heat, the fog, the anxiety — they were all connected. No one said, "This is a hot flash. This is estrogen leaving. This is why your focus and memory are glitching. Instead, I was told my tests were "normal." No explanation. No curiosity. When I said, "I'm not sure if I'm having a heart attack or a hot flash," no one blinked. No reassurance, no conversation — just another "normal" result.

So, I assumed it must be me. If the tests were fine, then maybe I was overreacting. If no one mentioned menopause, it must not be that. And when no one responded to my confusion, I started to wonder if I was just… losing it.

Even with all my professional training, I didn't see it — the intersection of menopause and ADHD. No one ever told me that when estrogen goes down, dopamine goes with it — that my brain wasn't failing; it was rebalancing. So, I kept blaming myself — for being scattered, unmotivated, emotional, even "lazy." I thought my ADHD had somehow gotten worse overnight. I thought my brain had forgotten how to be mine.

It took fear, confusion, and way too many unnecessary medical tests before I finally realized: I wasn't broken. My hormones were just having a staff meeting I wasn't invited to — and my doctors apparently weren't speaking to each other either. If I, a mental-health professional, could miss it — and my doctors weren't talking to each other, or to me — how many other women are sitting there thinking they're broken too?

WHY I WROTE THIS BOOK

Because no one told me what was happening — and I thought I should have known. Because too many women are sitting in exam rooms and therapy offices right now, terrified, exhausted, and misdiagnosed. Because when menopause meets ADHD, it's not just symptoms — it's identity. Even if they do understand what is happening little if any relief is offered.

We talk about menopause as a physical change. Even for women without ADHD, most doctors never explain what's really happening or what to expect — they just hand over lab results and tell you it's "normal" If they tell you anything.

We talk about ADHD as a neurodevelopmental condition and Perimenopause as a biological condition. But we almost never talk about what happens when those two collide inside the same brain — a brain that has spent decades compensating, performing, and trying to appear "together." When estrogen starts to dip, dopamine — the neurotransmitter responsible for motivation, reward, and focus — goes with it. And when dopamine drops, the ADHD brain, which already runs on a shortage of it, gets hit harder than most. The result, your usual coping skills stop working. Your memory, your mood, your focus, your motivation — everything that's been hanging by a thread — suddenly gives out.

This book is here to tell you it's not your fault. You are not weak. You are not undisciplined. You are not losing your mind. You're experiencing a brain-body shift that deserves understanding, not shame. And understanding is the first step toward getting your life (and focus) back.

HOW THIS BOOK WORKS

Each chapter blends science, story, and real talk to help you understand what's happening in your brain, your hormones, and your day-to-day life. I wrote it the way I wish someone had written something for me — practical, compassionate, and a little bit fun.

Think of this book as part therapy toolkit, part neuroscience crash course, and part late-night group chat where everyone's a little tired but still cheering each other on. Take what works for you right now and leave what doesn't. Then, when your journey through ADHD + menopause evolves, come back. There will always be something here waiting to meet you where you are.

To keep things simple, you'll see the same tools pop up throughout — each with a clear purpose and personality. At the end of every chapter, you'll find a "Putting It Into Practice" section. This is where you take the ideas you just learned and gently apply them to real life — no perfection required.

Here's what you'll find in each of the 4 sections.

- **What We Learned**

  A quick, clear summary of the chapter's most important points, plus a validating explanation of what they mean for you. This page reduces shame and connects the science to your lived experience.

- **Try this! Therapeutic tool**

  A simple, structured, ADHD-friendly worksheet designed to help you use the chapter's concepts in daily life.

- **Reflection + Integration**

  Therapy-style prompts and space to journal, so you can connect the dots and notice patterns with kindness (not criticism).

- **Mini Tools + Resources**

  Quick wins you can use even on low-capacity days — plus one research-backed resource to support your understanding.

These workbook pages are your scaffolding. They're the part of the book you can write in, photocopy, revisit, or ignore and return to later. There is no wrong way to use them. They're simply here to support your brain — especially on the days when nothing feels predictable.

MIND-BODY TOOLKIT

TOOL	PURPOSE	SAMPLE
Focus Fuel	To give actionable, evidence-based micro-strategies that restore energy, motivation, and attention when executive function is low	When restless: move it! A walk or stretch resets your brain's energy circuit. Motion feeds focus.
Hormone Lab Notes	Explain the science behind hormones, neurotransmitters, and how they shape real-world symptoms.	When estrogen dips, dopamine signaling falters. That's not laziness — that's chemistry.
Kelly Says	To connect professional insight with lived experience — using humor, humility, and storytelling to remind readers they're not alone in the process.	"If you can't find your focus, start by finding your glasses. Then your coffee. Then maybe your will to function."
Partnering with Providers	To build confident self-advocacy, helping to communicate with healthcare teams, ask informed questions, and co-create treatment plans.	Ask: "Could hormonal changes be affecting how my ADHD medication works?"
Therapist's Notes	To bring psychological insight to shifting thoughts, moods, and behaviors.	What looks like laziness is often masking—the mental effort of trying to appear "together."
Truth Bomb	To replace self-criticism with truth and humor that help you reset perspective.	"I don't call it impulsive; I call it being decisively enthusiastic."

→ If you've ever said, "I swear my brain used to work," you're in the right place.

→ If you've ever been told you're too emotional, too distracted, too tired, or too much — this book was written for you.

→ You are not losing control. You're learning how your brain works in a new season of life.

→ You're not broken. You're becoming more informed, more compassionate, and more powerful than you've ever been.

You're not alone. And you're definitely not crazy — not clinically, anyway. You're just living through the most under-discussed plot twist in women's mental health — and I'm right here with you, sticky notes, fan, and all. Let's turn the page — your brain's got stories to tell.

Part I: The Collision Course, Understanding What's Happening

I Used to Have It Together… Mostly

There was a time when I could juggle ten things at once. Well, maybe not gracefully, but the balls stayed in the air. Now I can't even remember where I put the balls. Or why I walked into this room. Or if I actually paid that bill—or just thought about paying it, which in my brain feels oddly similar. Sometimes I open the fridge, stare inside, and completely forget what I'm looking for.

Spoiler: it's usually motivation.

If this sounds familiar—if you've been wondering when your brain switched operating systems without warning—congratulations. You've entered the thrilling intersection of ADHD and menopause. It's not a midlife crisis; it's a midlife *rewiring.* And nobody warned us about it. To understand why everything feels harder now, we need to rewind a bit—to the wiring that's been there all along.

In the past I could juggle ten balls at once. Now I can't remember where I put the balls.

1: Before You Blame Yourself... Let's Talk About ADHD

ADHD isn't a lack of discipline or effort. It's not a personality flaw. It's a brain that runs on interest instead of importance. A neurotypical brain says, "This bill is due tomorrow, better pay it." An ADHD brain says, "This bill is boring… so I'll alphabetize the spice rack instead."

ADHD is rooted in dopamine regulation — the neurotransmitter responsible for motivation, reward, and focus. When dopamine dips, your ability to start, stick with, or finish a task

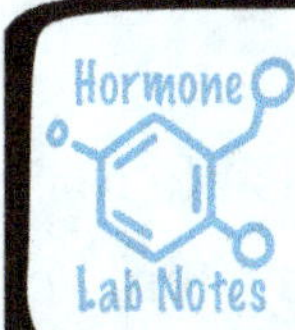

often drops right along with it. That's why an ADHD brain can hyperfocus on something fascinating for six hours yet completely forget a dentist appointment that's been on the calendar for three months.

It's not disorganization — it's dopamine economics. So, if you've always been a little scattered, creative, forgetful, or prone to starting ten things and finishing none — congratulations: you're not lazy. You're neurologically wired for curiosity, not consistency.

THE NEUROBIOLOGY OF ADHD

ADHD is a neurobiological condition, not a willpower issue. Research consistently shows measurable differences in brain structure, chemistry, and connectivity.

Neurotransmitter Differences

People with ADHD often have lower levels or less efficient activity of:

- Dopamine
- Norepinephrine

These chemicals regulate motivation, reward, attention, and emotional control.

Brain Regions Affected

Neuroimaging studies show differences in:
- Prefrontal cortex (planning, prioritizing, decision-making, impulse control)
- Striatum/basal ganglia (reward processing, motivation, task initiation)
- Cerebellum (movement + cognitive coordination)

These are the same regions responsible for executive functioning — the "management system" of your brain.

Connectivity Differences

White matter pathways (the brain's wiring) often develop differently in ADHD, slowing communication between focus, planning, and emotional-regulation networks.

Genetics

ADHD is one of the most heritable mental-health conditions (60–90%). Variants in genes related to dopamine receptors, dopamine transport, and neurotransmitter regulation are strongly associated with ADHD. ADHD is biological, measurable, and real — not a failure of discipline or character.

ADHD SUBTYPES: THE THREE WAYS CHAOS SHOWS UP

While ADHD shares a common core — challenges with attention, impulse control, and regulation — it doesn't look the same for everyone. The Diagnostic and Statistical Manual of Mental Disorders, 5th Edition (DSM-5) defines three main presentations:

Inattentive Type (a.k.a. *"Where Did My Brain Go?"*)

Hyperactive–Impulsive Type (a.k.a. *"The Subtle Kind"*)

Combined Type (a.k.a. *"Both Gears, No Brake"*)

Think of them as three flavors of the same sundae — different toppings, same base ingredient: a brain that needs dopamine to focus, and interest to stay engaged.

Inattentive Type Symptoms (a.k.a. "Where Did My Brain Go?")

Inattentive ADHD is the quiet, easily overlooked presentation — the one that hides in plain sight. Instead of bouncing off the walls, this version is more like your thoughts quietly slipping out the back door while you're trying to focus.

It's losing track of what you were doing, what someone just said, or why you walked into a room in the first place. For many women, this subtype feels like running through fog: you're trying, you're thinking, you're doing your best — but the mental picture keeps fading before you can grab it.

And because it's subtle, people often mistake it for stress, anxiety, or being "scatterbrained," when it's really your brain running low on the neurotransmitters that help you hold information steady.

Common patterns may include:

- Losing the thread in conversations or tasks.
- Difficulty organizing plans, priorities, or next steps.
- Chronic forgetfulness (appointments, deadlines, essentials).
- Starting things easily but struggling to follow through.
- Avoiding boring or repetitive tasks even when you *want* to do them.

Inattentive ADHD isn't about not caring or not trying. It's a brain that's wired to respond to interest, novelty, or urgency — not routine. When the dopamine signal is low, the mental spotlight flickers, and the simplest tasks feel slippery: you know what to do, you *want* to do it… and yet your brain quietly drifts away. This is not a character flaw. It's a neurological pattern that has probably been with you your whole life, finally making sense now that you understand how your mind actually works.

Hyperactive–Impulsive ADHD in adults rarely looks like the stereotype of bouncing off walls or running laps around a classroom. Instead, it's an internal hum that never quite shuts off, a fast-moving mind paired with emotions that leap before you have time to catch them.

This subtype often feels like the volume knob in your brain is turned up just one notch too high. You *look* calm on the outside, but inside it's a swirl of quick decisions, quick reactions, quick thoughts, and quick regrets.

It's not drama, and it's not "being too much" — it's your nervous system running on a faster setting than the rest of the room.

Common patterns may include:

- An internal sense of restlessness even when sitting still
- Talking quickly or interrupting without intending to
- Making fast decisions before fully considering consequences
- Overexplaining or filling silence because pauses feel uncomfortable
- Emotional reactions that flare fast and fade just as quickly

Women with this presentation often blame themselves for being "intense," "sensitive," or "impulsive," when what they're really feeling is their brain processing stimuli at full volume. It's a nervous system that reacts quickly — sometimes faster than you can redirect — and then leaves you replaying the moment long after everyone else has moved on. This isn't you being difficult. It's your ADHD showing up in a form that's less visible but just as real — and often deeply misunderstood.

Combined Type Symptoms (a.k.a. "Both Gears, No Brake")

Combined Type ADHD is what happens when the inattentive brain
and the hyperactive–impulsive brain
share the same space. It's the push–
pull feeling of wanting to go, wanting
to stop, and not quite knowing which
system is driving at any given

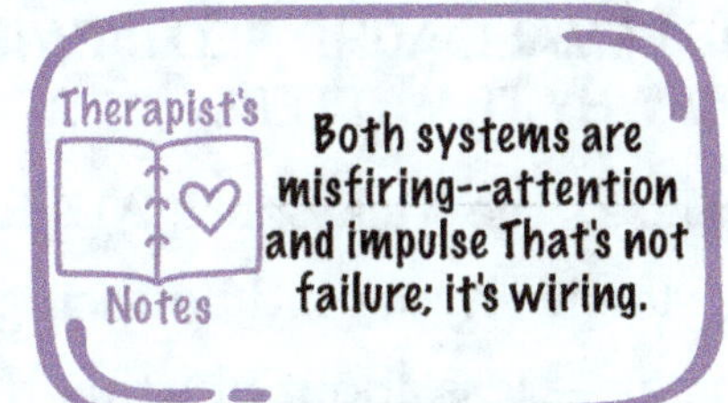

moment. For many adults — especially women — this presentation
finally explains the confusing mix of being mentally foggy *and*
mentally overstimulated. It's the sensation of having two engines
inside one mind: one revving too fast, the other stalling out. You try to
slow down and can't, try to speed up and something sputters. It's not
inconsistency — it's internal conflict.

Common patterns may include:

- Trouble following instructions or keeping track of multi-step
  tasks
- Chronic disorganization even with genuine effort
- Restlessness or fidgeting paired with mental fatigue
- Talking quickly or interrupting without meaning to
- Quick bursts of motivation that disappear just as quickly
- Both foggy focus and racing thoughts in the same day (or
  same hour)

Combined Type feels like running two software programs at the
same time that weren't designed to work together. You may start a
project impulsively (hyperactive brain), only to lose momentum
halfway through (inattentive brain). You may feel physically restless
while mentally drained, or mentally energized while your body feels
slow. It's the classic "go-go brain, slow-slow body" loop — and it's
exhausting.

This isn't laziness, lack of discipline, or mixed signals. It's a brain
running two competing operating systems, each one demanding
attention. Your job isn't to choose one speed — it's learning how to

shift gears without blaming yourself for the friction you were never taught to understand.

THE FEMALE ADHD PLOT TWIST: THE PART, NOBODY TOLD YOU — AND WHY IT MATTERS

Here's the tricky part: ADHD in women doesn't always look like the classic "hyper kid bouncing off the walls." For most women, it's quieter — less about blurting things out and more about juggling too much, dropping balls, and blaming yourself for it.

You may have spent years thinking, "I'm just bad at focus, organization, or time management. In reality, you've likely been living

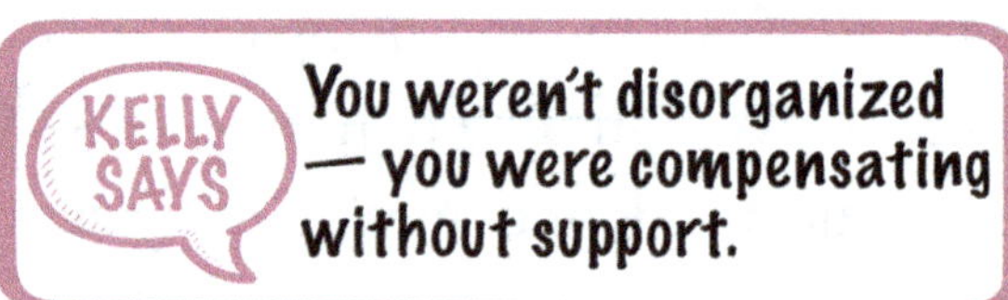

with the inattentive or combined presentation of ADHD — forms that are harder to spot and often mislabeled as anxiety, depression, or "just stress." While the hyperactive, impulsive version grabs attention, the inattentive kind quietly drains energy and confidence. It's the mental tabs you can't close, the lists you keep rewriting, and the appointments you swear you'll remember — but don't.

Women with ADHD are often experts at masking, compensating, and overworking to appear "together." But when hormones shift — like during perimenopause — those coping systems start to crumble, and the symptoms that were once hidden finally demand to be seen.

Women tend to mask symptoms through:

- Perfectionism
- Over-functioning
- People-pleasing
- Taking on more than they can manage
- Suppressing overwhelm until it becomes burnout

You may have spent years thinking:

- "I'm disorganized."
- "I'm inconsistent."
- "I'm too emotional."

- "I should be able to handle more."

You were living with ADHD — undiagnosed, unsupported, and constantly compensating.

Girls and women are **three times less likely** than boys to be diagnosed

Not because they have less ADHD — but because they show it

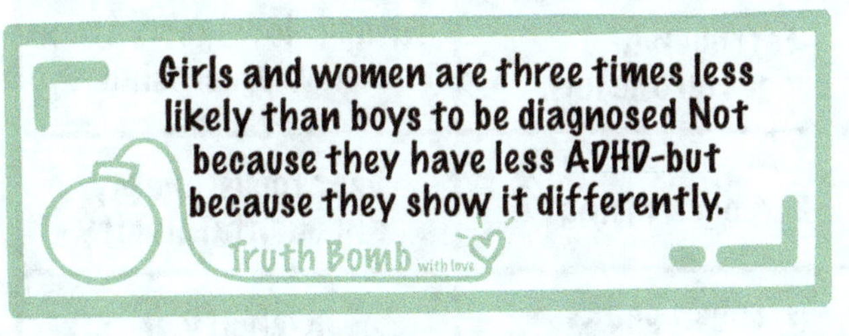

differently. – And then there's the part almost no one talks about:

Female hormones dramatically change ADHD symptoms — <u>every single month.</u> Your ADHD doesn't stay the same. It rises and falls with estrogen and progesterone because those hormones influence dopamine, norepinephrine, and serotonin — the exact neurotransmitters that ADHD relies on. This explains why some weeks you're sharp, motivated, and organized… and other weeks everything feels harder for reasons you can't explain.

How Hormones Shape ADHD Symptoms Throughout the Month

- Estrogen: The Helper. Estrogen boosts dopamine and serotonin. When estrogen is rising or high, women often experience:
  - Better focus
  - Improved mood
  - More motivation
  - Stronger executive functioning
- Progesterone: The Complicator. When progesterone rises in the second half of the cycle, it can blunt estrogen's benefits:
  - Brain fog
  - Irritability
  - Forgetfulness
  - Emotional swings
  - Medication feeling "weaker"

Women with ADHD are also at higher risk for Premenstrual dysphoric disorder (PMDD), because their neurotransmitter systems

ADHD Across the Monthly Cycle

Cycle Phase	Hormone Pattern	Impact on ADHD
Menstruation (Day 1)	Estrogen and progesterone low.	Fatigue, low motivation, slow processing
Follicular Phase (Day 6-14)	Estrogen rising	Best focus, energy, and mental clarity
Ovulation (day 14)	Estrogen peaks then drops.	Intensity or impulsivity may rise
Luteal Phase (Day 15-28)	High progesterone. Estrogen still high, but pre-ovulation. FSH and LH decrease.	Worsening symptoms: fog, overwhelm, irritability, emotional dysregulation

are already sensitive. Understanding your monthly cycle can help you replace self-blame with insight — and adjust expectations with compassion.

Where We Go Next

Monthly hormone shifts influence ADHD significantly — but perimenopause and menopause introduce a *bigger* shift. Instead of predictable cycles, estrogen becomes inconsistent, then declines. When estrogen drops, dopamine drops. When dopamine drops, ADHD symptoms intensify. This is where ADHD, hormones, and identity collide.

<u>WHAT WE LEARNED</u>
KEY INSIGHTS

- Estrogen directly supports dopamine, attention, working memory, and emotional regulation.
- As estrogen fluctuates, executive function becomes less reliable — not because you're failing, but because your brain shifted.
- Emotional reactivity increases because your stress-regulation circuits have less hormonal support.
- Old coping systems stop working because they were built for a different neurochemical landscape.
- This is not "you falling apart." It's your brain asking for updated conditions.
- Understanding the biology reduces shame and increases clarity.

WHAT THIS MEANS FOR YOU

You're not losing your abilities, discipline, or motivation — you're losing the hormonal support those abilities were built on. The shifts you're noticing are not personal failures. They're the natural result of your brain working without the steady estrogen that once buffered your attention, memory, stress circuits, and emotional regulation.

Your symptoms are real, valid, and explainable. This isn't you "falling apart." It's your brain recalibrating under new internal conditions. Once you understand the biology behind what's happening, things begin to make sense again — and shame has less room to grow. You don't need to push harder; you need tools that work with the brain you have today. That's exactly what this workbook section helps you build.

TRY THIS: THE DAILY CAPACITY CHECK

A 60-second reset to help you work with the brain you have today.
Use it in the morning and again mid-day when needed.

STEP 1 — NAME YOUR EMOITIONAL STATE

Circle or write one:
Foggy • Wired • Scattered • Emotional •
Low Motivation • Overwhelmed • Steady
Other: _______________________________

STEP 2 — PICK YOUR CAPACITY BANDWIDTH

Low Capacity – Minimal tasks, gentle expectations

Medium Capacity – A few structured tasks + breaks

High Capacity – One bigger task with time boundaries

STEP 3 — MATCH THE ACTION TO THE CAPACITY

If Low:

☐ One micro-task

☐ Reduce one step

☐ Lower expectations to 60%

If Medium:

☐ Choose 2-3 priorities

☐ Schedule breaks

☐ Remove friction

If High:

☐ Tackle one big item

☐ Set a time limit

☐ Leave buffer in your day

Try This Script:

**"This is what my brain can do today.
I'm working with it, not against it."**

Putting It Into Practice

Reflection & Integration

REFLECTION PROMPTS

- Where did I blame myself for something that was actually neurological?

- Where could I lower friction instead of raising pressure?

- What surprised me most about the estrogen-executive function connection?

JOURNAL SPACE

Helpful Insight

**"This isn't a character flaw. It's physiology.
You're learning new working conditions."**

Mini Tools & Resources

Mini Tool 1
Small wins for tough days. What are your wins today?

Mini Tool 2
Three-Item To-Do List

1.

2.

3.

Mini Tool 3
Two-Minute Reset
☐ Stand up
☐ Drink water
☐ Deep breath
☐ Stretch 20 seconds

Mini Tool 4
Overwhelm Pause

"Is this a demand, or a decision?"

PERIMENOPAUSE: THE TRANSITION NO ONE PREPARED YOU FOR (A.K.A. "WHY IS MY BODY DOING THIS AND WHY IS EVERYONE SO CALM ABOUT IT?")

Before we dive in, here's the simple version: This chapter explains what perimenopause actually is, what it does to your hormones, why your brain feels different, and why none of this is a sign that you're

failing. We're going to make this as clear, compassionate, and human as possible — with a little humor, because otherwise the absurdity might swallow us whole.

If you've ever stood in the grocery store staring at a shelf of pasta, completely unable to remember what you came for — not stressed, not distracted, just blank — you've already experienced one of perimenopause's calling cards. And if you've ever asked yourself, "Why am I suddenly sweating?" or "Why am I crying?" or "Why does everyone breathe SO LOUDLY?" … welcome. You're not alone, and you're not losing your grip. You're entering the transition that no one tells women how to navigate.

Perimenopause is the stage before menopause — the long, unpredictable transition where estrogen and progesterone stop following their lifelong schedule and start behaving like teenagers with a curfew they no longer respect. Most women don't realize this shift begins in their 40s, sometimes earlier. Even fewer have been told that perimenopause, not menopause itself, is where the real upheaval happens.

It doesn't announce itself with a dramatic moment. It starts small. A cycle that arrives a few days early… or late. PMS that feels bigger. A night of sleep that doesn't restore you the way it used to. You blame stress, exhaustion, aging, or maybe your own "inconsistency," because

no one ever explained that this stage even exists — let alone what it does to the brain.

Perimenopause is a physiological transition, not a personal failing. It is not your willpower slipping. It is not you "falling apart." It is your hormones doing something very normal — but very disruptive — for the first time in decades.

THE TRANSITION

Perimenopause can last years. Early on, cycles simply shift. Later, they become irregular — sometimes shorter, sometimes longer, sometimes disappearing entirely only to return with dramatic flair. In the late stage, hot flashes and night sweats begin to nudge their way into your nights. Emotional stability wobbles. Cognitive clarity flickers. And that stable internal sense of I know who I am may feel less reliable.

This is all part of the process. And no, it does not look the same for every woman. Your best friend may breeze through it with mild warmth and a few skipped periods. You may feel like you're riding a hormonal Tilt-A-Whirl. Both are normal.

Once you reach twelve straight months without a period, you're officially at menopause — a

single day on the timeline — and then post-menopause, where hormone levels stay consistently low. But the rollercoaster? That's perimenopause.

Why Hormones Stop Following the Script

To understand why this transition feels so personal, it helps to know how smoothly your system worked before now. For decades, your hypothalamus, pituitary gland, and ovaries communicated with the precision of a group text among best

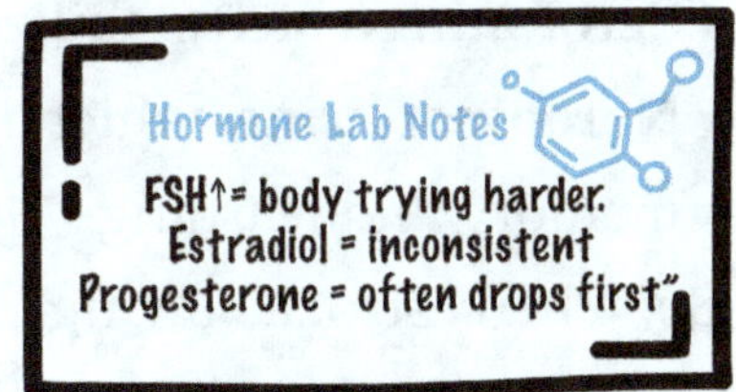

friends: predictable, coordinated, and full of clear instructions.

In perimenopause, the ovaries begin missing the message. They don't produce hormones as consistently. They don't respond to stimulation the same way. They sometimes send back mixed signals. Your brain perceives this as confusion and begins increasing its hormonal messaging — especially FSH (Follicle-Stimulating Hormone) — to try to get the ovaries back on track. Sometimes this works, resulting in a surge of estrogen that's unexpectedly high. Other times the ovaries don't respond at all, and estrogen drops. This instability is why your cycles, mood, sleep, energy, and overall sense of stability begin to wobble. It is not randomness — it is the hormonal feedback loop recalibrating.

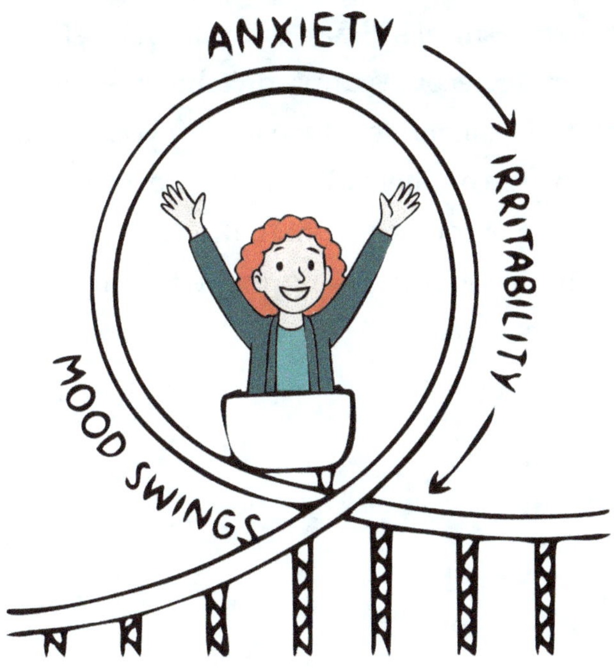

The Estrogen Rollercoaster

Here's the part nearly no woman has been told estrogen isn't just about reproduction. It is deeply involved in brain function. Estrogen supports four key neurotransmitter systems:

- **Dopamine**, which helps you focus, initiate, and feel motivated
- **Serotonin**, which stabilizes mood and emotional balance
- **Norepinephrine**, which influences alertness and attention
- memory and learning

So, when estrogen swings, these systems swing with it and when those systems swing, you feel it. Some days you may feel sharp, energized, and emotionally steady — that's a good estrogen day. Other days you may feel foggy, irritable, forgetful, or emotionally fragile — that's a drop or fluctuation. This isn't inconsistency in character. It's inconsistency in neurochemistry.

What About Progesterone?

Progesterone normally has a gentle, calming effect — helping you sleep and smoothing mood. But in perimenopause, progesterone is often the first hormone to fade. Without its steadying influence, emotional sensitivity increases. Falling asleep becomes harder. Stress tolerance shrinks. Small frustrations feel bigger. And because ovulation becomes unpredictable, the progesterone you do produce can feel exaggerated. One month you're mellow; the next you're crying because a commercial featured a dog in a sweater.

None of this is a moral failing.

This is the sidekick hormone turning its volume up and down at random.

Why Sleep Starts Falling Apart

Sleep disruption is one of the hallmarks, why does this happen mark symptoms of perimenopause, and it deserves its own moment here because it is one of the most misunderstood. Declining progesterone makes it harder to fall asleep. Fluctuating estrogen disrupts temperature regulation, triggering hot flashes and night sweats that wake you up abruptly. Mood changes make relaxation harder. And once you start waking up multiple times a night, your brain's ability to recover drops. And that means the next day you may have trouble focusing, remembering, regulating your emotions, or handling everyday stress.

This is not weakness. This is what happens when your sleep architecture is repeatedly disrupted. Why Your Medications Feel Different.

Another under-discussed part of perimenopause is how it affects medication metabolism. As estrogen and progesterone fluctuate, they influence the liver enzymes that process most medications. Some drugs may clear your system too quickly and feel less effective. Others may linger longer and feel too strong. This can happen with many medications — antidepressants, anti-anxiety meds, sleep medications, pain medications, seizure medications — and yes, ADHD medications as well.

If your meds suddenly feel inconsistent in your 40s, it's not because you are inconsistent. It's because your biology is changing and dragging your neurochemistry with it.

(We'll talk about the ADHD collision in the next chapter — this is just the groundwork.)

The Emotional Shift No One Warns You About

Emotional changes in perimenopause aren't random personality glitches. They have a biological explanation. When estrogen fluctuates, your emotional regulation systems fluctuate too.

You may find yourself more:

- irritable
- anxious
- tearful
- overwhelmed
- sensitive to rejection
- reactive to stress

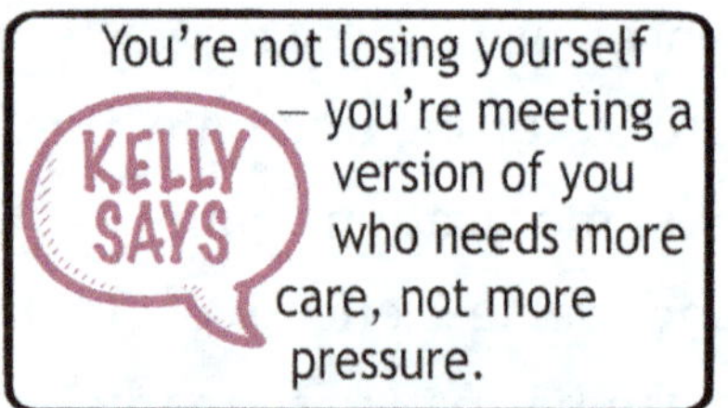

This isn't "being dramatic." This is a known period of emotional vulnerability — like PMS and postpartum — when estrogen swings rapidly and the brain struggles to adapt.

It's not in your head.

Well… it is. But not in the way people mean when they dismiss you. This is neurobiology, not fragility.

And Then There's the Brain Fog

Brain fog scares women more than almost any other symptom because it feels so sudden and so intrusive. One day you're articulate and on top of things; the next you're searching for words and forgetting why you opened your email.

Let's be clear: brain fog in perimenopause is not dementia.

It's not decline. It's not permanent.

It happens because estrogen supports memory and cognitive clarity, and when, that support becomes unstable. Once hormones stabilize again — which they do — cognitive clarity returns.

Your brain is not disappearing.

It's adjusting

A Moment of Reassurance

As chaotic as this feels, most symptoms improve when hormones settle into their postmenopausal baseline. Your brain recalibrates. Your sleep finds a new rhythm. Your emotional stability returns. And your sense of self — the real you — becomes easier to access again.

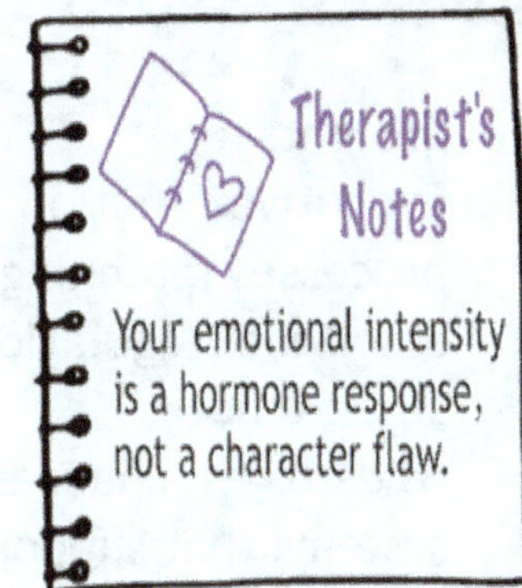

Every woman's experience is different.

Yours does not need to match anyone else's for it to be real.

Where We Go From Here

Now that you know what perimenopause is doing to your hormones and your brain, the next chapter tackles the part no one talks about: why women with ADHD feel these changes more intensely, more unpredictably, and often longer — and what actually helps. You're not losing your edge. You're moving through a transition that affects everything from neurotransmitters to emotional resilience. And your brain, even on its foggiest day, is still yours.

PUTTING IT INTO PRACTICE

<u>What We Learned</u>

Key Insights
- Executive function is not one skill — it's a network of mental processes (planning, initiation, sequencing, working memory, emotional regulation) that all fluctuate with hormones and stress load.
- As estrogen changes, the dopamine and norepinephrine systems that support these skills become less consistent — meaning your brain works harder to do the same tasks.
- Multitasking isn't real; it's rapid task-switching, and it drains energy much faster in midlife.
- Cognitive friction increases when your brain is overwhelmed — everything takes more steps, more reminders, more emotional effort.
- Mental load (the invisible planning and anticipating you do all day) skyrockets in this stage of life and is often completely unsupported.
- You're not becoming less capable — you're becoming less *resourced*. Your brain is carrying more weight with fewer internal supports.

What This Means for You

You are not suddenly disorganized or scattered. You are not failing to "keep up." You're carrying more tasks, decisions, emotions, and responsibilities than ever before — with a brain that no longer has the same chemical support behind it. Your executive function hasn't stopped working; it's overloaded. The problem isn't you — it's the mismatch between what life demands and what your brain is currently equipped to manage. The way forward isn't pushing harder. It's reducing friction, simplifying steps, and building support systems that work with the brain you have now. That's exactly what these next pages help you do.

Try This: The Cognitive Load Map (Part 1)

A gentle worksheet to help you see where your mental load is heavy — and where your brain needs support.

STEP 1 — List the Areas Holding the Most Weight

Write 3-6 areas that feel mentally heavy right now. These can be concrete (work deadlines) or invisible (holding everyone else's details in your head).

____

____

____

____

____

____

STEP 2 — Mark the Load Level for Each

Circle one per line:
Low / Med / High / Overloaded
Low / Med / High / Overloaded
Low / Med / High / Overloaded
Low / Med / High / Overloaded
Low / Med / High / Overloaded
Low / Med / High / Overloaded

STEP 3 — Choose ONE Area to Simplify

Pick the one that drains you most. Not the "should." The honest one.

Area: ________________________________

TRY THIS: The Cognitive Load Map (Part 2)

STEP 4 — Do a Friction Scan

Check all that apply to the area you chose:
- Too many steps
- Too many interruptions
- Too much remembering required
- Takes too long to restart
- Too many decisions
- Too much emotional energy
- Too many unknowns
- Drains me before I even begin

STEP 5 — Reduce Friction With ONE Change
Choose one small shift that makes the area easier:
- Remove a step
- Combine steps
- Lower the standard
- Automate something
- Delegate something
- Time-block a tiny window
- Change the timing
- Use a repeating reminder
- Ask for help
- Other: ___________________

Your one friction-lowering change:

____

____

Try This Script

"My brain isn't overwhelmed because I'm failing.
It's overwhelmed because it's carrying too much.
I'm allowed to make this easier."

Try This: Sequencing Support Page

A companion tool for starting tasks when your brain feels stuck.

The One-Minute Sequencing Trick

Ask:

"What is the first visible step?"
Not the whole task.
Not the outcome.
Just the first physical action.

Write it here:

____

____

Starter Steps Prompt

If your brain still freezes, choose one:

- Open the thing
- Lay out what I need
- Write one line
- Move one item
- Put the task in front of me
- Set a 2-minute timer
- Tell someone "I'm starting"
- Break the task into two steps

Identity-Friendly Reminder

You don't have to finish the task.
You just have to begin.
Momentum is the miracle, not perfection.

<u>Reflection + Integration</u>

Reflection Prompts

- Which part of my executive function feels least supported right now?

- Where am I defaulting to multitasking when my brain needs sequencing?

- What invisible task am I carrying that no one else sees?

- What small shift could make tomorrow feel 5% easier?

Journaling Space

Helpful Insight

"It's not that you can't do it. It's that you've
been doing too much, for too long,
with too little support."

PUTTING IT INTO PRACTICE

<u>Mini Tools + Resources</u>

Mini Tool 1 — The Stop Doing List

Your brain cannot carry everything. Write one thing you're not managing today:

I am not doing:

____

____

Mini Tool 2 — The 20% Rule

Ask: "What would this look like at 20% effort instead of 100%?" Then do *that*.

Mini Tool 3 — Overwhelm Interrupter

When your brain floods:
"Pause.
Is this a demand... or a decision?"

Mini Tool 4 — Working Memory Helper
Write the 2 things you want to remember for the next hour:

____

____

____

Resource Highlight
Give Your Brain One Safe Landing Spot

Pick one place — a notebook, a notes app, a paper pad — where everything goes.

Not organized. Not sorted. Just captured. This one shift reduces cognitive strain and keeps your brain from constantly scanning for what it might be forgetting.

3: When ADHD and Menopause Collide

(The moment your brain says, "Absolutely not.")

There's a certain kind of bewilderment that hits women with ADHD in midlife. It's the moment you look around at the undone tasks, the swirling thoughts, the emotional spikes, and the half-finished coffee you meant to reheat an hour ago — and think, "My life has always been a little chaotic… but this? This is different."

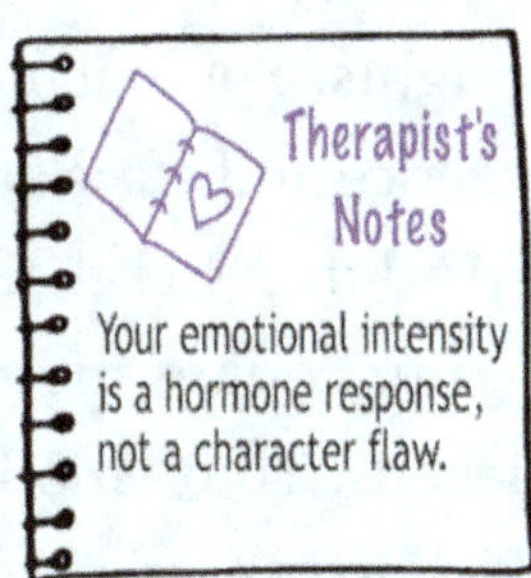

It often starts quietly; with questions you didn't expect to ask. Why am I more distracted? Why can't I start anything? Why does my patience evaporate? Why do tiny problems feel enormous? Why is my memory slipping? Why does my medication work beautifully one week and disappear the next?

And then the most frightening question:

"Is my ADHD getting worse?"

Let me be clear: your ADHD didn't suddenly intensify. Menopause arrived and began interfering with the very systems your ADHD relies on. This isn't failure. It's not a lack of discipline. It's a collision — biochemical and predictable, even if no one ever told you it was coming, The internal landscape you've spent a lifetime learning to navigate feels unfamiliar.

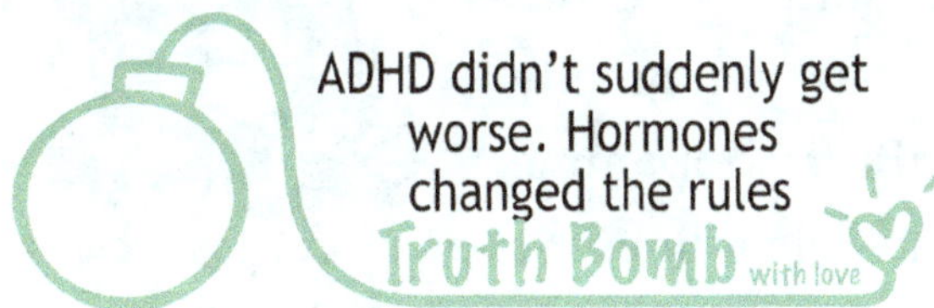

THE DOUBLE IMPACT (YOU TRULY AREN'T IMAGINING THIS.)

ADHD already shapes how your brain handles planning, attention, emotional regulation, memory, and momentum. And over time, you've built a whole ecosystem of coping strategies — some structured, some creative, some barely held together with sticky notes and hope — but they *worked*. They kept your life in motion.

Then perimenopause arrives, quietly at first.

It begins with subtle shifts: a little more irritability, a little more forgetfulness, a little more "Wait… why did I walk in here?" You misplace your phone. You misplace your thoughts. You misplace the second half of your sentence and stare at the wall trying to retrieve it.

And then the change becomes undeniable.

Your coping strategies don't land the way they used to. Brain fog thickens. Your emotional buffer starts to thin. You drop tasks you've effortlessly carried for years. Everything feels heavier, like life increased its difficulty setting without warning. Sometimes what you're feeling is ADHD. Sometimes it's hormones. Often, it's both at once, tangled together in ways that are hard to unravel. This isn't you "slipping." This is what happens when a dopamine-challenged brain meets fluctuating estrogen.

THE SCIENCE THAT FINALLY MAKES IT MAKE SENSE

No one tells women this, so let's say it plainly: Estrogen supports dopamine. Dopamine regulates ADHD symptoms. And during perimenopause, estrogen doesn't simply decline — it swings wildly. For decades, estrogen quietly supported four key neurotransmitters: dopamine, norepinephrine, serotonin, and acetylcholine. It helped keep motivation, attention, mood, and memory functional.

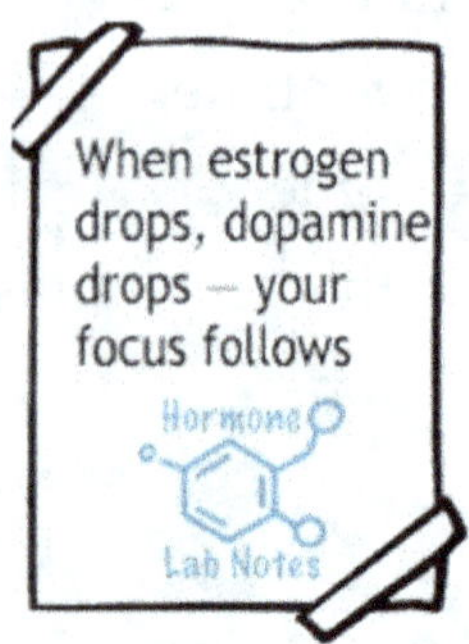

Then perimenopause begins. Estrogen rises, falls, spikes, and crashes — often in the span of days. And because ADHD already involves lower baseline dopamine, your brain feels these hormonal shifts immediately.

When estrogen dips, dopamine dips.

When dopamine dips, ADHD symptoms spike.

Which is why your brain feels slippery… your emotional fuse shortens… your frustration tolerance shrinks… And yes — this is why your ADHD medication can feel inconsistent, like it works perfectly on Monday and not at all by Friday. It's not you. It's the biochemical systems your medication relies on shifting underneath you.

WHY IT FEELS SO PERSONAL

Women describe this phase with almost haunting similarity:

"I used to function in chaos. Now I can't function at all."

"My brain feels glitchy."

"I'm crying constantly."

"I don't recognize myself."

It can feel as though the scaffolding that used to hold your life together is suddenly unstable. Starting tasks becomes harder than ever. Working memory slips. Emotional regulation weakens. Your stress tolerance shrinks. Masking — the thing you've done your entire life to appear competent and composed — life to appear competent and composed — becomes exhausting. And beneath all of that is the identity piece no one talks about.

It's not just your focus changing. It's how you see yourself. The version of you who could juggle, pivot, multitask, and power through feels far away. The confidence you once had in your ability to "pull it together" starts to wobble.

But this shift is biochemical, not personal.

You are not unraveling.

You are not becoming less capable.

You are moving through a neurological transition you were never taught to expect

WHAT THIS COLLISION LOOKS LIKE DAY-TO-DAY

These moments show up in everyday life:

A woman bursts into tears in the paper towel aisle because she can't decide between two brands.

Another opens her laptop six times in a row and forgets why each time.

Another sits in her driveway for an hour because she can't transition into the next task.

Another says her medication works "like magic on Monday and like air on Friday."

These aren't character flaws or failures. They're symptoms — predictable ones — and they make perfect sense once you understand the biology behind them.

WHY DOCTORS MISS THIS OVERLAP

Most clinicians were never trained to recognize the ADHD–menopause intersection. ADHD in women was underdiagnosed for decades. Menopause research is still catching up. Almost no studies examine the overlap. Emotional symptoms get mislabeled as depression or anxiety. Cognitive symptoms get dismissed as "normal aging." Medication inconsistency is rarely explained. So, when you say you're more distracted, more overwhelmed, more emotional, or less functional, you may get a sympathetic shrug — or a suggestion to "reduce stress."

Which leaves women thinking:

"What is wrong with me?"

"Why can't I focus the way I used to?"

"I should be able to handle this."

But here's the truth:

Nothing is wrong with you.

You're experiencing a biochemical collision between dopamine and estrogen.

WHERE WE GO FROM HERE

Now that you understand what's happening inside your brain, things start to make sense. You see why everything feels harder. You see why your tools aren't landing the way they once did. You see why your brain feels different than it used to.

In the chapters ahead, we'll walk through what actually helps — the supports, strategies, treatment options, and collaborative steps with your providers that stabilize the ADHD–menopause overlap. We'll talk about medication adjustments, restoring clarity, rebuilding energy, strengthening mood, and, most importantly, reclaiming trust in yourself.

You are not broken.
You are not "too much."
You are not falling behind.

You are moving through a scientifically explainable, biologically predictable transition that millions of women experience. Your ADHD didn't suddenly intensify — it's the part almost no one talks about.

Now that you understand the terrain, you can navigate it with clarity, confidence, and compassion.

What We Learned

Key Insights

- ADHD and menopause don't merely overlap — they interact, magnify each other, and create symptoms that feel dramatically different from anything you've experienced before.
- Estrogen has been quietly supporting dopamine, norepinephrine, serotonin, and acetylcholine for decades. When it begins to fluctuate, the scaffolding that holds up your attention, mood, memory, and motivation becomes unstable.
- ADHD brains already operate with lower baseline dopamine, so hormonal shifts hit harder, faster, and more unpredictably.
- This is why your medication becomes inconsistent, your emotions feel raw, your tolerance shrinks, and tasks you've carried for years suddenly feel unmanageable.
- What you're experiencing is not decline — it's a neurological transition no one taught you to expect.
- When symptoms intensify, it affects not only your focus and energy but also your **identity**, your confidence, and the way you see yourself.

WHAT THIS MEANS FOR YOU

Nothing about what you're experiencing is a personal failure. You're not losing abilities, discipline, or strength — you're losing the hormonal stability that used to support your brain behind the scenes. The overwhelm, the emotional surges, the forgetfulness, the slowed transitions, and even the "I don't feel like myself" moments aren't signs of unraveling. They're signs of a system in flux.

You're moving through a phase where symptoms feel louder, coping strategies feel weaker, and your sense of self may feel shaky. But this is biochemical, not personal. Your brain hasn't stopped working — it's working under new conditions. With the right support and tools, you can adapt to this internal shift with clarity and compassion.

Try This: The Symptom vs. Self-Separator Map (Part 1)

A grounding tool to help you distinguish between what is happening biologically and what belongs to your identity. Midlife symptom changes often get tangled with self-blame. This worksheet helps you separate the two so you can respond with clarity, not shame.

STEP 1 — NAME THE MOMENTS THAT FEEL HARD

List 3-6 things you've struggled with recently (memory, mood swings, task initiation, overwhelm, irritability, emotional spikes, mental fog, inconsistency):

1.
2.
3.
4.
5.

STEP 2 — IDENTIFY THE STORY, YOU TELL YOURSELF

For each item, write the automatic thought or self-judgment that shows up. Examples: "I'm so inconsistent," "I should be able to handle this," "I'm slipping," "What's wrong with me?"

1.
2.
3.
4.
5.

<u>Try This: The Symptom vs. Self-Separator Map (Part 2)</u>

STEP 3 — Identify the Likely Biological Cause

Choose all that apply:

- Hormonal fluctuation
- Emotional regulation shifts
- Sleep disruption
- Stress load
- Masking fatigue
- Nervous system exhaustion
- Estrogen drops → dopamine drops
- Medication inconsistency
- Working memory overload
- Cognitive fatigue

Rewrite each symptom with its biological explanation:
1.
2.
3.
4.
5.

STEP 4 — REWRITE THE NARRATIVE WITH COMPASSION

Replace the old interpretation with a kinder, more accurate one. Example: Old "I'm losing it."   New: "My dopamine dipped and my brain is doing its best with fluctuating support."

Your new interpretations:
1.
2.
3.
4.
5.

Try This Script
"This isn't a character flaw. This is a neurological shift.
I deserve support while my brain adjusts."

Try This: Identity Re-Anchoring Support Page

When symptoms change, self-perception changes. This page helps reconnect you with the parts of you that remain steady.

Mini Exercise — What Hasn't Changed About You?

List 3-5 qualities, strengths, or patterns that remain true:

____

____

____

____

____

Mini Exercise — What This Season Is Teaching You

Write 2-3 things you're learning about your needs, limits, or strengths:

____

____

____

____

Identity Grounding Statement

Complete the sentence: "I am still someone who…"

____

____

____

Momentum Reminder

> You haven't lost yourself.
> Your brain is adapting.
> Your identity is expanding, not disappearing.

Reflection + Integration

Reflection Prompts

1. Which recent struggles felt personal but might be biochemical?

2. Where did I assume "I should handle this" instead of recognizing overload?

3. What part of my identity feels shaken by these changes?

4. What new compassion do I want to offer myself moving forward?

Journaling Space

Helpful Insight

"Nothing about this makes you less capable. It only means your brain needs new conditions, not new criticism."

PUTTING IT INTO PRACTICE

<u>Mini Tools + Resource Highlight</u>

Mini Tool 1 — The 60-Second Dopamine Reset
Choose one:
- Light movement
- Cold splash on face
- Brief sunlight exposure
- Music that energizes
- Change rooms
- 10 slow breaths

Mini Tool 2 — Emotional Fuse Extender
Before reacting, try:

"Pause.
What is my brain chemistry doing right now?"

This one question slows the emotional spike.

Mini Tool 3 — Medication Tracker (Tiny Version)
On days it feels "off," note:

Today it felt:

- Strong - Okay - Weak - Absent

Mini Tool 4 — The "Good Enough Today" Standard
Name one thing you did today that was enough:

____

____

Resource Highlight
Identity-Friendly Reminder:
"You are not losing who you are.
You are meeting a new version of your brain —
and she needs different support

Part II: What To Do About It, A Team Approach

I finally understood what was happening in my brain.
Great.
Fantastic.

And then the next question hit me square in the face:

"Okay… so now what?"

Because knowing *why* your brain feels like a browser with 47 tabs open is helpful — but it doesn't magically close any of the tabs. Or help you remember where you put your keys. Or stop you from crying over the wrong brand of paper towels.

Understanding is the first step. But the real relief comes from knowing what to **do** about it — what actually helps when ADHD and menopause team up and start rewriting your neurological settings.

And here's the truth no one tells you:

There is **no single fix.**
Not one doctor.
Not one medication.
Not one strategy, supplement, or planner page.

This is a whole-brain, whole-body, whole-life transition.
Which means the support needs to be whole team.

In Part II, we're bringing together a multidisciplinary lineup — medical providers, therapists, ADHD specialists, sleep experts, nutrition experts, daily systems, and practical strategies that actually work in real homes with real humans… not theoretical unicorn routines. This is where things start to feel doable again. Manageable. Supported.

You've made sense of the collision. Now let's talk about how to rebuild your traction — one clear, evidence-based, real-life tool at a time.

Partnering With Your Provider
Special expanded tool

Understanding your needs. clarifying your symptoms, and preparing for appointments.

What are you experiencing (check all):

- Trouble initiating tasks
- Increased overwhelm
- Brain fog/losing words
- Executive function crashes
- Forgetfulness/memory lapses

- Medication feeling inconsistent
- Mood swings or emotional spikes
- Longer recovery time after stress
- Sleep disruptions

- Emotional sensitivity / thin buffer

What You Want Help With Today?

- Changing ADHD symptoms
- Medication adjustments
- Perimenopause symptoms
- Mood or emotional regulation
- Testing or evaluation

- Sleep issues / fatigue
- Anxiety or irritability
- Cognitive fog
- Hormone interactions
- Lifestyle questions

How These Symptoms Affect Daily Life

(Providers use this to determine treatment needs.)

- Work / focus
- Relationships
- Communication

- Stress tolerance
- Emotional regulation
- Time management

- Routines
- Motivation
- Stress tolerance

Examples (optional but helpful):

- "My medication feels strong one week and weak the next."
- "I lose momentum halfway through the day."
- "I react emotionally faster than I can catch it."

Your goals

- Better focus
- Lowering overwhelm

- Improved sleep
- More day-to-day stability
- Understanding ADHD vs. hormonal shifts

- Finding the right meds/ dose
- Adjusting treatment for hormones

- Building sustainable routines
- Reduced emotional reactivity

What 'better' would look like for me:

Understanding your needs. clarifying your symptoms,
and preparing for appointments.

What To Ask Your Provider

Medication & Hormone Interactions

"My medication feels different throughout the month — can we explore why?"

"Are there adjustments we can make during high-symptom weeks?"

Symptom Patterns

"These symptoms are new for me: ______."

"These symptoms have intensified: ______."

Treatment Options

"Are there alternative medications or add-ons that might help?"

"Could hormone therapy be appropriate?"

"What do you recommend for sleep issues in ADHD + perimenopause?"

Clarifying What's Normal vs. Concerning

"Which symptoms are typical for perimenopause?"

"Which symptoms should we monitor closely?"

Scripts for Hard Conversations

If You Feel Dismissed

"This is affecting my functioning, not just my feelings."

"Can we slow down and explore options together?"

"How are you coordinating care with my other providers?"

If You Need Clearer Explanations:

"Could you explain that in simpler terms?"

"How will we know if this treatment is working?"

If You Feel Overwhelmed:

"Can you summarize the main next steps before we wrap up?"

"Can we pause for a moment?"

WHEN THE RULES QUIETLY CHANGE

I knew something had shifted the morning I sat at my kitchen table staring at my ADHD medication bottle like it had personally betrayed me. Normally this tiny pill is my ignition switch. My "okay brain, let's do this" moment. But that day? Nothing. No clarity. No spark. Just a dull static, as if someone had unplugged half my neurons and walked away.

My first instinct was to blame the pharmacy. My second was to assume my brain had developed sudden medication immunity. And my third—the one I didn't want to say out loud—was: Is this menopause again? Is it really messing with me this much?

What I didn't know then is what so many women eventually learn the hard way: midlife quietly rewrites the body's operating instructions. Treatments that had been reliable for years suddenly feel unpredictable. Routines stop landing the way they used to. Sleep patterns shift without your consent. Emotional steadiness bends. Cognitive traction slips. And you start wondering if your ADHD treatment stopped working—or if your biology has simply changed.

The truth is: **it's both.**

You didn't fail.

Your treatment didn't fail.

Your brain's environment shifted, and the tools that fit your old terrain may not fit the new one.

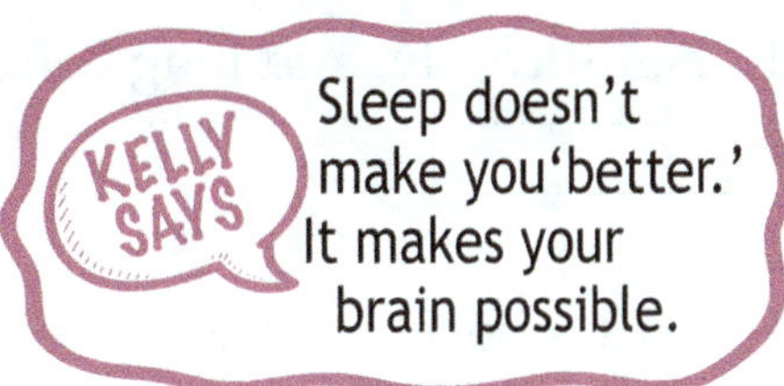

WHY HORMONES HIJACK YOUR CLARITY

Estrogen has been quietly stabilizing your brain chemistry your entire adult life. You may not have known it, because it never announced itself. It simply supported the systems that regulate motivation, focus, emotional steadiness, memory, and cognitive fluidity.

When estrogen begins fluctuating, the systems it supports fluctuate too.

Dopamine becomes less predictable.

Norepinephrine signaling becomes less smooth.

Working memory falters.

Emotional regulation feels thinner around the edges.

Women describe it in ways that sound emotional, but underneath is biology:

"I don't trust my brain the way I used to."

"My meds don't feel the same."

"Everything feels heavier."

This isn't weakness.

It's chemistry.

Menopause doesn't tap you on the shoulder and ask if you're ready.

It simply changes the internal landscape—quietly, significantly, and long before any lab test catches up.

Medical support becomes more important now not because you're falling apart, but because your brain deserves care that matches the season you're living in. Think of it as driving a familiar car on a very different road. The car isn't broken. The driver isn't failing. The suspension just needs adjusting because the terrain changed.

HORMONE THERAPY: WHAT IT CAN (AND CAN'T) DO

Hormone therapy carries a reputation it didn't earn and expectations it can't meet. Some women hope it will bring back the version of themselves they miss. Others fear it because of outdated research or confusing headlines. The truth—as usual—lives in the middle.

Hormone therapy does **not** treat ADHD.
But it absolutely stabilizes the systems that ADHD depends on.

When estrogen becomes more consistent, many women notice steadier moods, clearer thinking, fewer catastrophic "crash days," and medication that behaves more predictably. Because estrogen influences dopamine sensitivity, supports the prefrontal cortex, and dramatically boosts BDNF (the brain's repair-and-resilience molecule), stabilizing estrogen levels can smooth the ride for your cognition.

But hormone therapy is not universal.
Not every woman needs it.
Not every woman is a candidate.
And not every woman experiences dramatic changes.

It is an option—a helpful one for many, a moderate one for some, and unnecessary for others. Knowing this helps set expectations that are hopeful, not magical.

Timing matters.
Delivery method matters.
And it works best as part of a team approach, not a standalone cure.

Hormone therapy stabilizes the terrain.
ADHD treatment navigates it.
You don't have to choose one or the other—they're complementary tools.

WHEN MEDICATION STARTS FEELING... DIFFERENT

One of the most disorienting parts of midlife ADHD is when medication that's been stable for years suddenly feels unfamiliar.

Some days it seems weaker. Other days it feels too sharp. Sometimes it fades too quickly. Sometimes it hits all at once. And sometimes it feels like it doesn't work at all. This doesn't mean your medication stopped working. It means the hormonal environment around it changed.

Estrogen directly affects stimulant sensitivity. When estrogen is higher, medication may feel smooth and consistent. When estrogen drops, the same dose may feel flat, short-lived, or oddly emotional. This change isn't a flaw in your treatment—it's a shift in your biology.

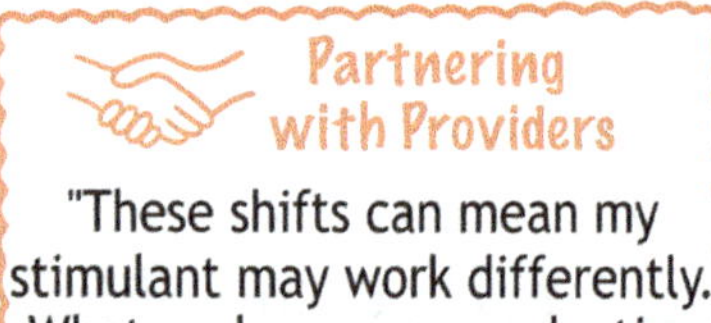

This is the phase when many women start believing something is wrong with them:

"I'm slipping."
"I'm getting more sensitive."
"Maybe I can't tolerate meds anymore."

But none of that is true.

Midlife often requires small recalibrations—adjusting timing, combining short- and long-acting doses, adding a small booster, or simply finding a formulation that feels smoother. These aren't restarts; they're tune-ups.

Your brain isn't misbehaving.

It's adapting to a new internal landscape.

WHEN STIMULANTS SUDDENLY FEEL TOO STRONG, OR JUST WRONG

There's a pattern I see constantly in midlife: women suddenly feel overstimulated by medication doses they've tolerated for decades. A familiar dose may now bring jitters, emotional sharpness, sensory overwhelm, or a feeling that everything is turned up one notch too high.

It's not that your medication became stronger.
It's that your nervous system became more reactive.

Estrogen influences emotional buffering and sensory tolerance, so when estrogen dips, the brain is simply more sensitive. You're not becoming "too emotional" or "overly reactive." Your system is running hotter, and medication is highlighting what hormones used to soften.

The solution isn't to abandon treatment.
It's to recalibrate around your new sensitivity:

Earlier dosing.
Smoother-release formulations.
Smaller increments.
More grounding before and after dosing.
Less caffeine.
More predictable meals.

This isn't fragility; it's physiology. And with the right adjustments, treatment feels predictable again.

THE STABILIZERS THAT HOLD EVERYTHING TOGETHER

This is the part women are most tired of hearing about—sleep, nutrition, and movement. Not because they're unimportant, but because they've been explained badly, wrapped in guilt, or handed out like moral obligations.

We're not doing that here.

Sleep, nutrition, and movement are not lifestyle upgrades.

They're biochemical stabilizers.

Sleep is the time your brain resets dopamine receptors and clears waste products that slow thinking. When menopause disrupts sleep—and it often does—your executive function, memory, and emotional regulation feel it immediately.

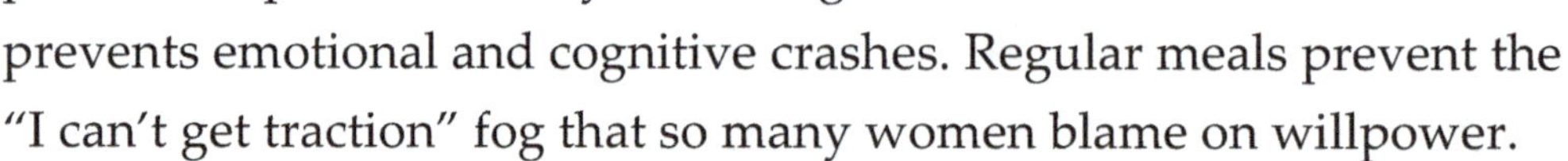

Nutrition is not discipline; it's neurotransmitter fuel. Protein helps produce dopamine. Steady blood sugar prevents emotional and cognitive crashes. Regular meals prevent the "I can't get traction" fog that so many women blame on willpower.

Movement is BDNF in action. Even ten minutes signals the brain to repair, adapt, and increase dopamine sensitivity. You don't need a gym—just a body willing to move.

These aren't rules.
They're supports.
They make your brain more capable.

INTEGRATIVE CARE WITHOUT THE NOISE

Midlife is the moment women often fall into one of two extremes: the "take these 14 supplements and detox your soul" camp or the "none of that matters" camp. The truth—unsurprisingly—sits somewhere in the middle.

Some integrative tools are genuinely helpful: omega-3s, magnesium, vitamin D when deficient, mindfulness practices, and light therapy for circadian rhythm shifts. These aren't fringe theories—they have decades of research behind them.

Other tools show promise but need more study: adaptogens, phytoestrogens, acupuncture, gut–brain strategies, and specific herbal supports. They can be wonderful additions when used with context and guidance.

And then there are the things that sound scientific but aren't: unvalidated hormone panels, supplement mega stacks, adrenal fatigue testing, and high-dose hormone pellets. These often create more chaos than clarity and leave women feeling like failures for not buying the right tincture.

Integrative medicine is most powerful when it supports your medical care—not replaces it. It fills gaps. It eases stress load. It helps your system regulate so that your primary treatments can do their job.

You deserve clarity, not overwhelm.

PUTTING THE MEDICAL STORY TOGETHER

If Part I explained why everything feels harder, this chapter is the part where things finally begin to feel doable again. You are not imagining your shifting needs. You are not high maintenance. You are not losing your mind. You are responding to a real biochemical transition—one that affects neurotransmitters, sleep cycles, metabolism, emotional steadiness, and executive function.

Medical treatment in midlife isn't about fixing you.

It's about meeting your changing brain where it is.

Your needs are allowed to change.

Your treatment plan is allowed to evolve.

Your brain is allowed to ask for help.

This isn't regression.

This is recalibration.

And now that you understand the terrain, you can move forward with tools that match the reality of your biology—not the expectations of who you used to be.

What We Learned

Key Insights

- Your ADHD medication didn't "stop working"—your hormonal environment changed, and medication depends on that environment.
- Estrogen has been quietly stabilizing dopamine, norepinephrine, serotonin, and acetylcholine for decades; when it fluctuates, your brain feels it immediately.
- Hormone therapy isn't a cure for ADHD, but it stabilizes the foundational systems ADHD relies on.
- Sleep, nutrition, and movement are not lifestyle boxes to check — they are biochemical supports that directly stabilize neurotransmitters.
- Integrative tools aren't magic or nonsense—they're helpful *when used alongside* medical care, not instead of it.
- You're not high-maintenance or falling apart. Your biology is shifting, and your medical treatment needs to shift with it.

What This Means for You

You didn't do anything wrong, and you're not losing the progress you've made. Your ADHD isn't worsening — your hormonal terrain is changing underneath your treatment plan. The medications, routines, or supports that once worked smoothly may now need recalibration, not because you failed, but because your brain's chemistry changed.

This stage of life often requires updated dosing, timing, sleep support, nutritional stability, or movement habits. Not as punishment — but because these interventions restore neurotransmitter balance in a system that's suddenly more fragile. Your brain is not misbehaving. It's asking for help that matches the reality of your biology.

Try This: Treatment Clarity Map (Part 1)

A simple worksheet to help you understand what's shifting — and what may need support.

STEP 1 — What Has Changed?

Check all that apply:

- Medication feels weaker
- Medication timing feels off
- Cognitive fog/slowed thinking
- More overwhelm
- Forgetfulness increased
- Energy crashes
- Lower motivation

- Medication feels too strong
- Mood feels less steady
- More irritability
- Trouble starting tasks
- Sleep harder to maintain
- Emotional spikes
- Increased sensory sensitivity

STEP 2 — When Do These Changes Happen?

Check or write in patterns:

- Certain times of the month
- After poor sleep
- In the afternoon/evening
- When stress piles up
- Around hot flashes/night sweats
- Randomly
- After skipping meals / blood sugar drops
- On low-estrogen days

Patterns I've noticed:

Try This: Treatment Clarity Map (Part 2)

STEP 3 — What Might Be Causing the Shift?

Circle all that feel relevant:
Hormones • Sleep disruption • Stress load
Blood sugar swings • Medication timing
Working memory overload • Estrogen dip
Nervous system fatigue • Medication absorption changes

STEP 4 — What to Bring to Your Provider

Choose 1-2 items to think about and process:
- Adjust timing
- Try short/long-acting formulations
- Consider a "booster" dose
- Evaluate transdermal estrogen (if appropriate)
- New plan for sleep support
- Look at blood sugar patterns
- Add magnesium or omega-3s (if safe)
- Track symptom variation

My top two:

1.
2.

Try This Script

"My medication didn't stop working —
my brain's environment shifted."

Support Page: The Stabilizers Map

A companion tool to help you reinforce the three systems that stabilize neurotransmitters during menopause.

These aren't "shoulds."

They are biochemical supports that directly help dopamine, norepinephrine, and BDNF function.

Sleep Stabilizer

Check one small shift to try this week:

- Dim lights earlier
- Keep the room cooler
- Reduce evening scrolling
- Try magnesium (if safe)
- Create a wind-down cue (lamp, blanket, scent)

Nutrition Stabilizer

Choose one:

- Eat protein with breakfast
- Add a mid-afternoon protein snack
- Reduce long gaps between meals
- Add one blood-sugar-friendly meal

Movement Stabilizer

Pick the easiest option:

- 5-minute walk
- Stretching
- One flight of stairs
- Light yoga
- Dance to one song

Stabilizing Reminder

These aren't about discipline.

They restore the chemistry your brain is missing.

<u>Reflection + Integration</u>

Reflection Prompts

1. What changes have I been blaming on myself that might be biochemical?

   —————————————————————————

2. Where have I tried to power through when my brain needed support?

   —————————————————————————

3. What part of my treatment plan might need adjusting during this season?

   —————————————————————————

4. What support would help me trust my brain again?

   —————————————————————————

   —————————————————————————

Journaling Space

Helpful Insight

"You don't need to push harder.
You need support that matches the biology you're living in."

PUTTING IT INTO PRACTICE

Mini Tools + Resource Highlight

Mini Tool 1 — Hormone-Aware Medication Check
Today my medication felt:

    ☐ Strong   ☐ Okay   ☐ Weak   ☐ Flat / Absent

Pattern tracking reveals biological shifts — not personal failures.

Mini Tool 2 — Blood Sugar Rescue
Try a "protein first" snack:

cheese • nuts • yogurt • eggs • jerky • tofu • cottage cheese

Small stabilizers → fewer crashes.

Mini Tool 3 — Emotional Buffer Builder
Before reacting, ask:

"Is this hormones... or me?"

This slows the fuse by anchoring you in biology.

Mini Tool 4 — 5-Minute Dopamine Reset
Choose one:

    ☐ Move for 60-90 seconds

    ☐ Step into fresh air

    ☐ Cold splash on face

    ☐ Upbeat music

    ☐ Change your environment

Resource Highlight
A Compassionate Reminder:

"Your treatment plan is allowed to evolve.
Your needs are allowed to change.
This isn't backsliding — it's recalibrating."

5: Mental Health Treatment

There's a moment almost every woman with ADHD hits in midlife. It never happens during a crisis. It happens during something tiny — a sock that didn't make it into the laundry basket, a text you meant to answer six hours ago, a partner asking a perfectly reasonable question at the wrong possible moment. Suddenly your reaction is bigger than the moment deserves, sharper than you expected, or more emotional than makes sense even to you. Afterward you sit there thinking, *Who even was that?* And then, I never used to react like this. What is happening to me? That gap — the distance between who you *feel* like and who you *remember* being — is where this chapter begins.

Because mental health treatment in midlife isn't about fixing flaws or learning how to "cope better." It's about understanding why everything feels different, why your emotional responses have shifted, and why strategies that worked for years suddenly feel like they're barely holding the seams together. This chapter isn't a list of techniques.

It's a map of what actually helps when ADHD, hormones, history, lived experience, and the realities of everyday life all collide. It's warm, grounded, clinically real, and meant for the woman you are now — not the woman you were at twenty-five.

WHY THERAPY MATTERS MORE DURING THIS PHASE

Midlife isn't just a hormonal transition; it's an emotional one. Estrogen doesn't simply affect hot flashes — it affects your brain's entire regulation system. For decades, estrogen has strengthened the communication between the prefrontal cortex (the reasoning, calming part of your brain) and the amygdala (the reactive, protective part).

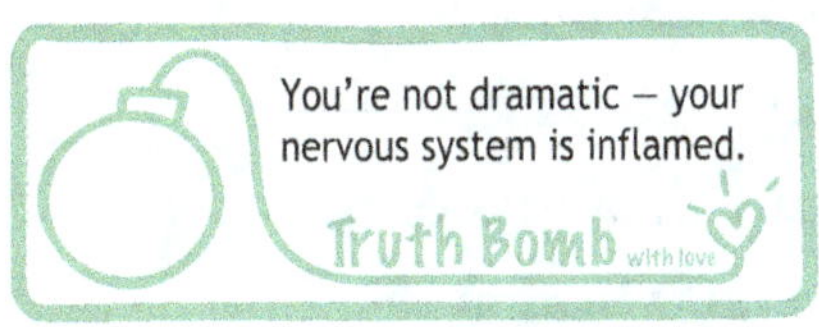

When estrogen fluctuates, that communication gets glitchy. Your emotional "buffer zone" — the space between stimulus and reaction — becomes thinner.

In real life, that looks like shorter patience, quicker tears, sharper irritability, and a sense that your reactions are happening *to* you, not *from* you. None of this is weakness. It's neurobiology interacting with stress, history, and lifelong patterns of coping.

Therapy becomes the place where you can sort through the noise. It helps you separate what is hormonal from what is emotional, what is historical from what is happening right now. It gives you a steady place to land while your internal system temporarily rewires itself.

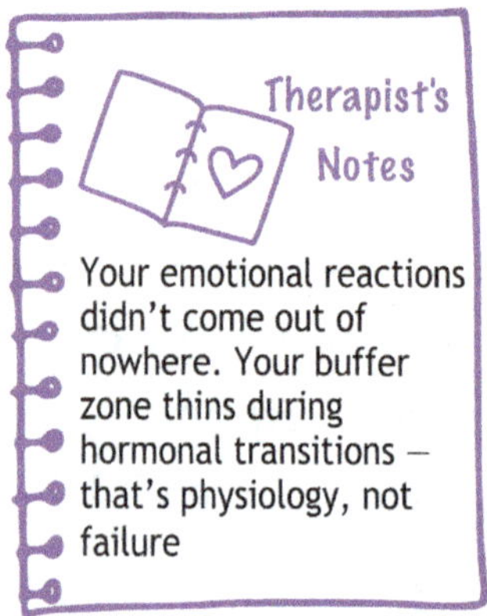

THERAPY APPROACHES THAT ACTUALLY HELP MIDLIFE ADHD WOMEN

Traditional therapy often misses the mark for women with ADHD — especially now. Many have spent decades being told to "try harder," "be more consistent," or "stop being so emotional." By midlife, those messages are baked into the internal critic.

But effective therapy for ADHD women doesn't demand more effort — it reduces unnecessary effort. It acknowledges the invisible labor you've carried, the expectations placed on you, the stress of masking symptoms, and the weight of roles you were never meant to manage alone.

Good therapy at this stage:

validates the cognitive and emotional changes

gives language to the chaotic internal experience

strengthens emotional grounding

builds systems that match your brain's actual needs

softens shame so you can access your strengths again

Most of all, it helps you understand yourself with compassion instead of criticism — an approach that ADHD brains respond to far better than pressure.

COGNITIVE-BEHAVIORAL TOOLS — BUT THROUGH A MIDLIFE LENS

CBT gets a bad reputation online because people often present it as: "Just change the thought!" But midlife ADHD brains are navigating hormonal intensity, emotional surges, sleep disruption, sensory overload, and cognitive fatigue. A worksheet won't magically calm that down.

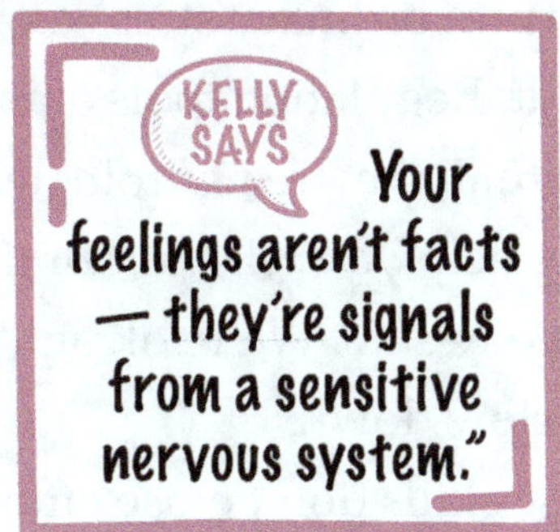

Real CBT — the kind seasoned clinicians use — looks very different. It becomes a way of gently noticing the stories that rise when you're overwhelmed:

the "I'm failing,"

the "Why can't I handle this?",

the "Everyone else seems fine."

It helps create a little space between the feeling and the meaning you assign to it. Not to erase the feeling — but to give you room to breathe and respond rather than spiral.

At this stage of life, CBT is softer, slower, more compassionate. It honors biology, not just behavior. It focuses on interrupting shame spirals, not correcting your personality. It helps you build tiny, repeatable habits that make sense for a brain that's more sensitive and less buffered. This is CBT rewritten for real life — and for real women.

MINDFULNESS AND NERVOUS SYSTEM REGULATION

Mindfulness in midlife isn't sitting still with an empty mind. It's noticing the internal surge before it becomes a tidal wave. It's catching the moment your chest tightens or your thoughts speed up. It's remembering that not every spike in emotion is truth — sometimes it's hormones, exhaustion, or overstimulation. Nervous system regulation becomes essential because fluctuating estrogen makes your brain interpret ordinary stress as threat. Regulation tools aren't spiritual; they're neurological. They help you tell your brain:

We're safe. We're okay. We can slow down.

These skills don't erase emotion — they make emotion navigable.

EXECUTIVE FUNCTION SUPPORT — REAL TOOLS FOR REAL BRAINS

By midlife, most women have built a patchwork of coping strategies — calendars, alarms, adrenaline pushes, late-night sprints, color-coded moments of inspiration. Those systems worked well enough… until they didn't. When hormones shift, executive function shifts with them. Therapy at this stage isn't about building the "perfect system." It's about lowering friction:

- Fewer steps
- Simpler routines
- Less working memory
- Supports that work even on low-capacity days

You're not rebuilding your personality.
You're designing environments that match your current brain.

Executive function support in midlife becomes the scaffolding that holds you up when motivation, stamina, or focus fluctuate. Tiny wins matter far more than complicated plans — and reducing friction is often more effective than increasing effort.

EMOTIONAL REGULATION AND BURNOUT RECOVERY

Midlife is often the point where emotional resilience feels stretched thin. Hormones amplify everything — the good, the painful, and the everyday irritations that suddenly feel enormous. Combine that with decades of invisible labor, internalized pressure, people-pleasing, perfectionism, and burnout becomes almost inevitable. But burnout in midlife isn't a failure of strength. It's a mismatch between what you've been carrying and the support you've been given. Therapy helps you rebuild emotional capacity by:

- Recognizing internal overload before it spikes
- Building slower, kinder responses
- Recovering from chronic stress cycles
- Creating space around emotions instead of suppressing them

Burnout recovery here isn't a vacation. It's reconstruction. It's restoring parts of yourself that haven't been centered in years. It's shifting from "pushing through" to "moving with support." This is the heart of midlife healing: giving your brain the space to reorganize instead of expecting it to perform like nothing has changed.

THE ROLE OF HUMOR AND SELF-COMPASSION

Humor is neurological medicine — especially now. It interrupts shame, calms your nervous system, and reminds you that you're not defective; you're human. Sometimes the most therapeutic moment is the one where you step outside a spiraling thought and say, "Okay… this is ridiculous, but I'm still here."

Self-compassion works the same way. ADHD brains don't thrive under pressure or criticism. They thrive under warmth, connection, and relief. Treating yourself kindly isn't indulgent. It is neuroscience. Kindness stabilizes emotional circuits, strengthens resilience, and helps your brain return to equilibrium. Midlife isn't asking you to be tougher. It's asking you to be gentler with yourself than you've ever been.

PULLING IT ALL TOGETHER

Mental health treatment in midlife is not about reinventing who you are. It's about understanding the woman you've become — a woman with decades of strength, creativity, and endurance, now navigating a brain in transition. Therapy helps you reinterpret your reactions: not as failures, but as signals. It helps you separate identity from biology, truth from temporary surges, patterns from stories. It reconnects you with the version of yourself that hasn't disappeared — she's just been overwhelmed.

You're not unraveling.
You're reorganizing.
And therapy gives you both the map and the companionship to move through this stage with steadiness.

The next chapter brings these internal insights into your daily world — the routines, environments, communication, and systems that help your brain function at its best.

PUTTING IT INTO PRACTICE

What We Learned

Key Insights
1. Emotional reactivity increases during midlife because estrogen fluctuations weaken communication between the amygdala and the prefrontal cortex.
2. ADHD already heightens emotional sensitivity, making hormonal shifts feel sharper and more overwhelming.
3. Old emotional patterns can resurface—not because you're regressing, but because your emotional "buffer zone" is thinner.
4. Therapy during midlife becomes a recalibration: separating biology from identity and giving your nervous system new support.
5. CBT, when adapted for midlife ADHD, becomes gentler, more compassionate, and more curious—not rigid or policing.
6. Mindfulness and nervous system regulation aren't abstract concepts — they're practical, science-backed ways to create space before your brain spirals.
7. Burnout in midlife ADHD is not a moral failing — it is the predictable result of decades of carrying more labor, more masking, more emotional management, and more responsibility with less internal support.

What This Means for You
You are not becoming someone new and unrecognizable — you are moving through a phase where your emotional system is more sensitive, your stress tolerance is lower, and your nervous system is stretched thin. Your reactions make sense. Your brain is not malfunctioning; it is recalibrating.

The strategies you used in your twenties or thirties may not fit anymore, not because you've "slipped," but because you're navigating a different internal landscape. Emotional surges, bigger reactions, or burnout aren't evidence of weakness — they're signals. And with the right tools, you can create space, anchor yourself, and respond in ways that feel more aligned with who you are. This workbook helps you do exactly that.

Try This: Emotional Surge Map (Part 1)

A tool to help you understand what's happening beneath an emotional spike.

STEP 1 — Identify the Moment

Write one recent moment where your reaction felt bigger than the situation:

STEP 2 — What Did You Feel?

(Choose all that apply)
- Overwhelmed
- Hurt
- Irritated
- Panicked
- Embarrassed
- Flooded
- Frozen
- Ashamed
- Exhausted
- "Not myself"

Emotion notes:

STEP 3 — What Triggered It (on the surface)?

- A comment
- A request
- A delayed task
- Something forgotten
- Something out of place
- A small mistake
- A sensory overload
- A minor inconvenience
- A tone or expression
- A mismatch in expectations

The trigger:

PUTTING IT INTO PRACTICE

Try This: Emotional Surge Map (Part 2)

STEP 4 — What Was Beneath the Reaction?
(Check all that apply)

Biological Layers
- Estrogen dip
- Poor sleep
- Hunger / low blood sugar
- Stress accumulation
- Sensory overload
- Medication inconsistency
- Exhaustion
- Overwhelm

Historical / Emotional Layers
- Old pattern resurfaced
- Feeling unappreciated
- Fear of disappointing others
- Old shame story
- Feeling alone in responsibility
- Perfectionism pressure
- Identity wobble

    Notes:

STEP 5 — Separate the Moment from Your Identity
Complete the sentence:

"What happened was…"

"What it meant about me was…"

Now draw a line through the second one. It's not your identity — it's a story.

Try This Script (Use During Surges)

"This reaction isn't who I am.
It's a combination of hormones, history, stress, and exhaustion.
I can give myself space before responding."

Try This: Midlife ADHD CBT Reframe Map
A gentle, compassion-centered reframing tool (not rigid CBT).

STEP 1 — What Story Did Your Brain Tell You?
(Example: "I'm failing," "Everyone's upset with me," "I can't handle anything.")

STEP 2 — What Else Might Be True?
Choose or write your own:

- My nervous system is overloaded.
- This feels bigger because my hormones dipped.
- I'm tired, not incapable.
- I've been carrying too much.
- My brain is protecting me, not punishing me.
- This moment is hard, but temporary.
- I can pause before deciding what it means.

What else might be true?

STEP 3 — A Kinder, More Accurate Reframe (Gentle, not forced)
"Given what my brain is navigating, this reaction makes sense. A softer version of the story is..."

STEP 4 — Choose One Supportive Response

- Step away for 2 minutes
- Drink water
- Eat protein
- Slow breathing
- Revisit conversation later
- Humor: "Okay, drama brain... relax."
- Text a friend
- Move to a quieter space
- Remind myself: "Different brain, different season"
- Rest my eyes

My choice:

<u>Reflection + Integration</u>

Reflection Prompts

1. What emotional patterns feel sharper during this phase of life?

2. Where have I mistaken a hormonal or neurological surge for a personal flaw?

3. What helps me create space before reacting?

4. What is one emotional narrative I'm ready to rewrite?

Journaling Space

Helpful Insight

"You are not overreacting — your brain is overwhelmed.
You're allowed to respond with compassion instead of criticism."

Mini Tools + Resource Highlight

Mini Tool 1 — 90-Second Nervous System Reset
If the surge is rising:
- Cold water on hands/face
- Step outside
- Hand over heart + slow exhale
- Light stretch
- Change rooms

Mini Tool 2 — "Name the Layer" Check-In
Ask:
"Is this biological, emotional, historical, or all three?"
Naming it gives you control.

Mini Tool 3 — Tiny Boundary Cue
When overstimulated, try:
"I need a moment — I'll come back."
Simple. Direct. Protective.

Mini Tool 4 — Humor Interrupt
When spiraling:
"Okay… this is ridiculous, but I'm still here."
Humor lowers threat signals.

Resource Highlight
A Gentle Reminder:

"Your emotional system isn't breaking —
it's speaking loudly.
You're learning how to listen without blaming yourself."

There is a strange, almost echoing silence around the overlap of ADHD and menopause. Not because it's rare — it isn't — but because the systems meant to support women rarely speak to each other. You can sit in your primary care office describing brain fog, emotional volatility, and focus issues, and walk out with a handout on stress. You can sit with a therapist explaining overwhelm, anxiety, and burnout, and never hear the word "estrogen." You

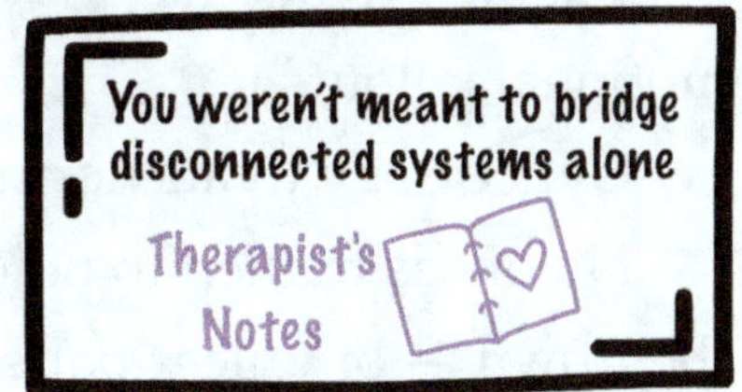

can speak to a psychiatrist about ADHD and still feel like you're the only one connecting your symptoms to your hormones.

Women become the bridge between disconnected forms of care — translating symptoms, searching the internet late at night, piecing together what should have been integrated from the beginning. And all of that is happening *while you're trying to navigate your own brain*. It's an enormous amount of invisible labor.

This chapter is about that intersection — the place women end up living by default. It's about the gaps between medical care, mental health care, and hormonal care. It's about the advocacy women are forced into and the changes we desperately need. And most importantly, it's about what to do while

we wait for the system to catch up.

WHY MEDICAL AND MENTAL HEALTH CARE MUST INTEGRATE

Hormones and neurotransmitters are part of the same ecosystem. Estrogen shapes dopamine and norepinephrine; dopamine shapes emotional regulation, executive functioning, and cognitive stamina. Sleep, stress tolerance, and memory are braided together through both systems. But healthcare still behaves as if the brain and the body live on different planets.

- Primary care treats hot flashes.

- Psychiatry treats ADHD.

- Therapy treats the emotional fallout.

- Gynecology treats hormones.

No one is trained to hold the full picture unless they learned it on their own — or unless patients force the conversation. Women pay the price for that fragmentation. They're asked to break down their symptoms into categories that don't reflect how those symptoms actually exist. They're told "that's normal," "that's stress," or "that's just age," when it is very clearly something more connected — something that deserves a multidisciplinary lens.

The truth is simple: ADHD and menopause are inseparable in the brain. But in medicine, they've been treated like unrelated events happening in separate bodies. Until that changes, women are left doing the integrating themselves, and that's a burden they were never meant to carry alone.

THE BARRIERS WOMEN FACE — AND THE WEIGHT THEY CARRY

Most women don't arrive at midlife with perfect diagnostic histories. They arrive with decades of misdiagnosis, underdiagnosis, or self-blame. They were the "daydreamer," the "sensitive one," the "disorganized mom," the "overworked professional," the "tired woman who just needed better habits." Their symptoms were mislabeled as stress, anxiety, depression, hormones, or personality quirks. So, by the time menopause hits and symptoms intensify, women often assume the problem is *them* — not their biology.

Clinicians do the same. Cognitive changes get brushed aside as aging; emotional intensity gets labeled anxiety; executive dysfunction gets attributed to stress or "doing too much." Women learn to mask, minimize, over-function, and keep moving. And when they finally seek help, they are often asked to *prove* their experience. The problem isn't that women aren't communicating clearly. The problem is that the system wasn't built to hear them.

WHY ADVOCACY MATTERS — AND WHAT IT REALLY MEANS

Advocacy sounds like a big, intimidating word, but in real life it looks like this:

- Asking a provider to consider the hormonal context.
- Naming the overlap out loud.
- Sharing your lived experience without apologizing for it.
- Saying, "This is all connected, and I need you to treat it that way."

Advocacy isn't about confrontation. It's about insisting that your full self is visible.

It's also about challenging the outdated assumptions that still shape research and clinical practice. Studies on ADHD were primarily done on boys and men. Research on menopause lagged for decades. Research on the intersection of ADHD and menopause is barely beginning. Women deserve better. Better studies, better clinical guidelines, better awareness.

But systemic change starts with women telling the truth about their experiences — to providers, to researchers, to each other. Every time you say, "This matters," you're pushing the system a little closer to catching up.

THE POWER OF COMMUNITY AND PEER SUPPORT

There is a type of healing that medicine cannot offer — the healing that comes from being in the presence of women who say, "Same here." Community removes the shame that isolation breeds. It normalizes the symptoms no one else seems to talk about. It gives you mirrors and language and anchors. It provides emotional oxygen.

You don't need a formal support group.
Sometimes community is one trusted friend.
Sometimes it's an online circle of women navigating the
same midlife plot twist.

Sometimes it's a group chat where everyone compares notes about sleep, meds, focus, and hot flashes. Community doesn't fix the symptoms. It makes them survivable. Because when women understand each other, they heal faster — not because someone solved the problem, but because someone finally *saw* it.

WHAT IT MEANS TO ADVOCATE FOR YOURSELF (WITHOUT BURNING OUT)

Women often hesitate to advocate because they fear being dismissed (or history of being dismissed), labeled as difficult, or judged. But advocating for care isn't a sign of being demanding. It's a sign that you're paying attention to your body and your brain.

Effective advocacy is grounded, calm, and clear:

- Here's what I'm noticing.
- Here's how it affects my life.
- Here's what I suspect is connected.
- Here's what I need you to consider.

You aren't asking for special treatment. You're asking for accurate treatment. Advocacy isn't about fighting. It's about clarity. It's about partnership. And it's about refusing to carry the integration labor alone

PULLING IT ALL TOGETHER

The intersection of ADHD and menopause is not a personal failure — it's a structural gap. The systems meant to support you were not trained to see the whole picture. You are living inside the consequences of that gap, not the cause of it.

But you're not powerless. Every insight you've gained, every pattern you've recognized, every moment you've trusted your own experience — all of it is advocacy. All of it is integration. All of it is a form of reclaiming your mental health.

You deserve coordinated care.
You deserve providers who listen.
You deserve support that matches the complexity of your lived reality.

And you deserve to move into the next chapter of this book — and the next chapter of your life — knowing that you're not alone, not dramatic, not imagining things, and not behind.

The next chapter translates this understanding into daily life — how to design routines, environments, and systems that support your real brain in a real world, especially when the world demands more from you than ever.

<u>What We Learned</u>
Key Insights

1. The healthcare system treats ADHD and menopause as separate worlds, even though they interact constantly in the brain.
2. Women are often forced to be the "bridge" between medical, hormonal, and mental health providers — an exhausting form of invisible labor.
3. Misdiagnosis, dismissal, and outdated assumptions mean women enter midlife with years of invalidated symptoms.
4. ADHD symptoms during menopause are not personal failures — they reflect changes in estrogen, dopamine pathways, emotional regulation, and cognitive load.
5. Integration isn't optional; women need coordinated support across primary care, psychiatry, therapy, and gynecology.
6. Community and peer support reduce shame and help women understand that they're not alone, not dramatic, and not imagining their symptoms.

What This Means for You

You were never meant to carry the burden of interpreting symptoms, translating medical language, and advocating between disconnected providers. You're not overreacting — you're living inside a system that wasn't built for midlife ADHD brains. Your experiences are real. Your symptoms make sense. And you deserve coordinated care that acknowledges your hormonal, neurological, and emotional reality. This section helps you identify what you need, communicate it clearly, and stop doing the integration labor alone.

Try This: Provider Advocacy & Care Integration Sheet

STEP 1 — What Do You Need Right Now?
Check all that apply:

- Clearer explanation of symptoms
- Hormone therapy discussion
- Emotional regulation guidance
- A therapist who understands ADHD
- Medication review
- Sleep support
- Executive function support
- A doctor who listens
- Validation that the ADHD-menopause overlap is real

My top 2 needs:

STEP 2 — Who Handles What?

Primary care handles:
Psychiatry handles:
Therapy handles:
Gynecology handles:
Other providers:

STEP 3 — What Do You Want Providers To Understand?
(Examples: "My symptoms change with hormones," "I need clear instructions," "I'm overwhelmed, not unmotivated.")

STEP 4 — Your Advocacy Talking Points
Choose 2-3 to use at your next appointment:

1.
2.
3.

Try This Script
"I'm noticing symptoms that cross between hormones and ADHD. I'd like us to look at this together instead of treating them separately."

<u>Reflection + Integration</u>
Reflection Prompts

1. Where have I been expected to integrate my own care?

2. What support do I need that I haven't asked for yet?

3. What assumptions about my symptoms have I internalized from the system?

4. Who in my life could be part of my community or support network?

Journaling Space

Helpful Insight

"You were never meant to navigate disconnected systems alone. Your experience is real — and you deserve coordinated care."

Mini Tools + Resource Highlight

Mini Tool 1 — Appointment Prep (30 Seconds)
Write one goal for the visit:

Mini Tool 2 — The "One Sentence Summary"
Use this to open any appointment:
"My symptoms change with hormones— I need you to consider that."

Mini Tool 3 — Community Check-In
Text one person:
"Hey, can we compare notes on what we've been noticing lately?"

Mini Tool 4 — The Validation Cue
Repeat:
"This isn't in my head. The system is behind. I'm not."

Resource Highlight
Connect with one ADHD-women-in-midlife community
(online or in person).

Hearing "me too" is often more
stabilizing than any medical advice.

There comes a point in midlife when you realize the systems you've relied on for years—your routines, your coping strategies, your color-coded calendars, your late-night second winds—don't quite fit anymore. Not because you're slipping or slacking or losing discipline, but because the brain running those systems is different now. The tools that once held your life together start feeling strangely heavy. The routines that once helped you feel organized feel overwhelming. The energy you always counted on is suddenly unpredictable. Women often respond to this shift the same way they've responded to every challenge their entire lives: by trying harder.

Trying harder to remember.
Trying harder to be consistent.
Trying harder to keep everything spinning.

But trying harder is a strategy that breaks down fast when hormone fluctuations destabilize the exact brain circuits responsible for planning, prioritizing, emotional buffering, and task initiation. Midlife isn't asking you to double your effort. It's asking you to redesign your environment, so it carries more of the load—so your brain doesn't have to.

This chapter is about that redesign. Not a reinvention of who you are, but a reimagining of the world around you so your life supports your brain, not the other way around.

WHEN OLD SYSTEMS STOP WORKING

One of the most confusing parts of midlife ADHD is how suddenly your previously reliable systems can collapse. You may find yourself staring at a planner that once made perfect sense and now feels like a foreign language. You may feel yourself bouncing between tasks with no traction. You might swear that your home shrank overnight because every room suddenly feels visually loud.

It's jarring.

It's disorienting.

And it's not your fault.

As estrogen fluctuates, the brain's ability to filter stimuli, shift attention, organize sequences, and regulate emotional energy becomes less predictable. The executive functioning system that helped you maintain routines becomes inconsistent. So, routines based on that system—routines that rely on memory, sustained energy, or uninterrupted attention—crack under the

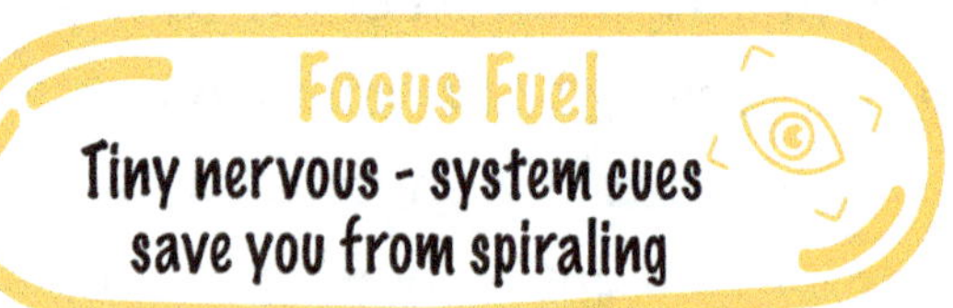

weight of fluctuating biology. But here's the part women aren't told, When the internal system shifts, the external system must shift with it. Not to compensate for weakness, but to align with a new operating reality. Midlife isn't the time to ask your brain to behave like it used to. It's the time to build an environment that behaves the way your brain needs now.

DESIGNING FOR THE BRAIN YOU HAVE TODAY

ADHD brains thrive when friction is low and cues are clear. But most women have been taught that reducing friction is "taking shortcuts" or "being lazy." Midlife reveals the truth: low friction is smart. Low friction is efficient. Low friction is how you keep yourself steady during hormonal turbulence. Designing a life that supports your brain is about building systems that work on

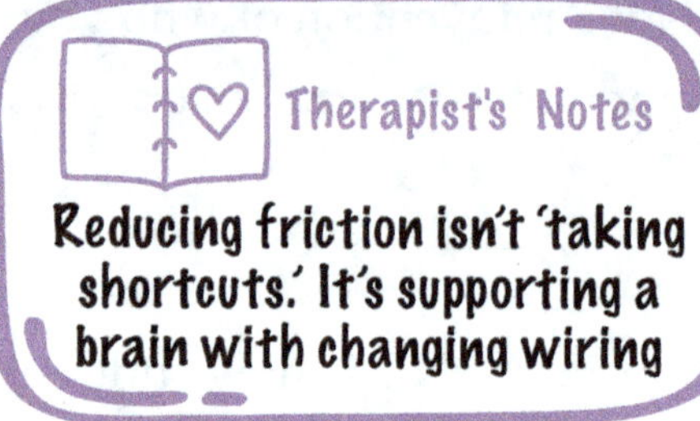

your lowest-capacity days—not just your highest ones. Because consistency doesn't come from motivation anymore; it comes from scaffolding.

Scaffolding isn't rigid or controlling. It's supportive. It's the structure around you that keeps you upright when internal conditions are wobbly. It's the difference between collapsing into overwhelm and having something to lean on. Realistic systems for ADHD + menopause don't demand more effort—they remove it. They don't require you to remember—they help you remember without trying. They don't pressure you—they protect you. This isn't about giving up. It's about adapting gracefully.

THE REAL WORK: LOWERING COGNITIVE FRICTION

The hardest part of midlife isn't the tasks themselves—it's the *activation* energy required to get to them. Women describe it as:

"It's like the air around me got thicker."

"I know what I need to do; I just can't seem to start."

"Everything feels like it takes more steps than it should."

"I used to be able to push through—now I feel stuck."

That's cognitive friction. And that friction increases dramatically during hormonal transitions.

Designing your life around your real brain means removing unnecessary steps wherever possible. Not to make things "easier," but to make them *possible.* When friction goes down, function goes up. When function goes up, shame goes down. When shame goes down, emotional regulation improves—and the entire day changes shape. Simplifying your environment isn't surrendering; it's strategy. It's acknowledging the truth: your brain has changed, and your systems need to catch up.

CAPACITY-BASED LIVING: THE NEW RHYTHM OF MIDLIFE

One of the most liberating shifts women make in this season is moving from expectation-based living to capacity-based living.

Expectation-based living says:

"I should be able to do what I used to do."

Capacity-based living says:

"I will choose what fits the brain I have today."

Capacity fluctuates now. Some days you have clarity. Some days feel foggy or wired. Some days are emotional. Some days you move slower. None of those days are failures. They're simply snapshots of your internal chemistry. When you design your life around capacity instead of pressure, you stop fighting with your own brain. You stop performing productivity. You stop collapsing under guilt. You start building rhythms that flow with your nervous system rather than crash against it. Midlife becomes far more navigable when you shift from "How do I push myself to do more?" to "What version of support does today's brain need?"

This isn't lowering standards.

This is living in alignment with reality.

REGULATING THE HOME ENVIRONMENT

In midlife, your external environment can either drain you or stabilize you. Visual noise becomes louder. Clutter becomes cognitively heavier. Decision-making becomes more taxing. Sensory input—lights, sounds, textures—can tip your nervous system faster than it used to.

Designing a supportive home doesn't mean becoming a minimalist or decluttering your entire life. It means noticing what overstimulates you and removing that friction gently. It means creating anchors—

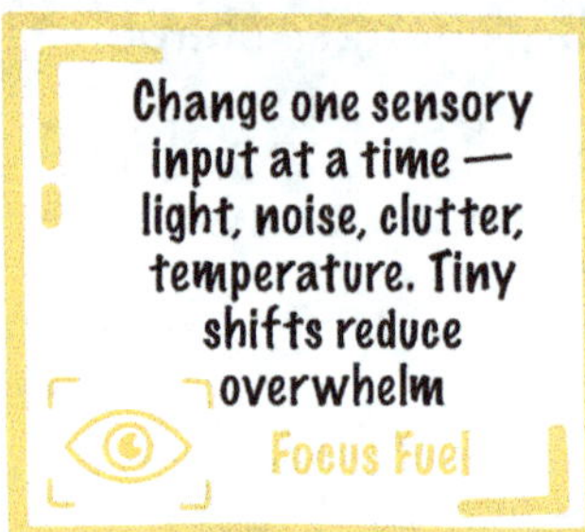

small, predictable cues that help your brain transition smoothly between parts of your day. It means building containers for things that used to live comfortably in working memory but now need physical support. This is nervous system design, not home makeover culture. Your home becomes an ally when the world feels loud.

COMMUNICATION THAT REDUCES LOAD, NOT INCREASES IT

Midlife symptoms don't just happen internally—they shape relationships. When your brain is foggy, emotional, overstimulated, or inconsistent, communication with others can feel harder. Partners and family members may misunderstand your changes as moodiness, distance, or disinterest. Designing a life that supports your brain includes designing communication that supports your relationships. It means being able to say:

"I'm overloaded; I need a moment."

"Today feels foggy; I'll need simplicity."

"This reaction is bigger than the situation; give me some space."

"My brain is doing the midlife thing again—nothing is wrong."

Not because you owe explanations, but because reducing misunderstanding reduces emotional labor. Clear, calm, compassionate communication lowers pressure on your internal system and improves connection instead of conflict. This isn't about excuses. It's about honesty—and honesty creates support.

ENERGY BUDGETING: THE HEART OF MIDLIFE FUNCTIONING

Midlife energy isn't linear. Some days you have a full tank. Some days you wake up with a quarter tank and don't know why. Some days your energy crashes suddenly at 2 p.m. without warning. ADHD already affects energy regulation; menopause amplifies it. Energy budgeting isn't about doing less. It's about investing your energy where it actually matters, preserving capacity for what's essential, and avoiding the patterns that lead to emotional blowouts or burnout spirals.

Your nervous system is asking for a different rhythm now. When you honor that rhythm, everything becomes more doable—not because life gets easier but because the way you move through it

becomes aligned with your biology. The goal isn't maximum efficiency; it's sustainable functioning.

LETTING GO OF SHAME AROUND SUPPORT

This is one of the most profound emotional shifts of midlife: letting yourself use support without guilt. ADHD women have spent decades being resourceful, flexible, hyper-responsible, and self-sufficient. Many have carried the mental load for entire families. Accepting support—organizational tools, reminders, conveniences, streamlined routines, even rest—can trigger old shame stories:

→ "I should be able to do this myself."

→ "Other people don't need this much help."

→ "I'm slipping."

→ "I'm becoming high maintenance."

None of that is true.

Using support is not weakness. Using support is adaptation. It's using the tools your brain deserves. It's honoring the realities of your neurobiology instead of pretending they don't exist. Menopause doesn't take your strength; it reveals the ways you've been doing too much with too little support for too long. Letting go of shame is part of healing.

PULLING IT ALL TOGETHER

Designing a life that supports your brain isn't about becoming someone new. It's about meeting the woman you are today with clarity and compassion. The systems you build now aren't punishment or compensation—they're alignment. They're acknowledgment. They're a love language for your nervous system.

You're not failing because you need different support.
You're evolving.
Your brain is shifting, and your life gets to shift with it.
When your environment stabilizes you, your emotions soften.

When your emotions soften, your cognition steadies.

When your cognition steadies, your confidence returns.

This chapter is about redesigning your life, so you don't have to fight your own brain just to get through the day. It's about creating a world that holds you—especially on the days when you feel unsteady.

In the next chapter, we bring everything together: the medical changes, the emotional shifts, the environmental support, the daily structures. You'll see how all of these pieces form a new kind of stability—one built not on pushing harder, but on understanding your brain as it is now and supporting it with every tool available.

What We Learned

Key Insights

1. Your midlife brain operates differently — systems that relied on memory, consistency, or energy no longer match your internal wiring.
2. Hormonal fluctuation increases cognitive friction, making old routines feel heavier and less reliable.
3. Supportive systems work by reducing friction and externalizing tasks rather than pressuring your brain to "try harder."
4. Capacity-based living is the new sustainable rhythm — expectations shift based on the brain you have today.
5. A supportive environment stabilizes your nervous system, improves transitions, and reduces emotional and cognitive overload.
6. Shame decreases and functioning increases when your environment and communication match your real capacity, not old expectations.

What This Means for You

You're not losing your abilities — you're navigating a brain with different internal settings. The routines and systems you've used for decades weren't designed for this hormonal landscape. You don't need stricter rules or more discipline. You need scaffolding — external supports that hold you steady when your internal wiring fluctuates. The work is not pushing harder. The work is aligning your life with your brain.

PUTTING IT INTO PRACTICE

Try This: The Cognitive Friction Audit
A tool for spotting where your life is draining your attention — and where redesign will help most.

STEP 1 — Identify One Area That Feels Hard Right Now
(Examples: mornings, email, transitions, laundry, bills, cooking, work startup.) Area: _______________________________________

STEP 2 — Where Is the Friction Coming From?
Check all that apply.

Cognitive Friction

- [ ] Too many steps
- [ ] Requires memory
- [ ] Feels visually loud
- [ ] Emotionally heavy
- [ ] Decision overload
- [ ] Hard to start
- [ ] No clear cue
- [ ] Requires sustained focus

Environmental Friction

- [ ] Clutter
- [ ] Noise
- [ ] Lighting
- [ ] No landing zone
- [ ] Items in wrong location
- [ ] Overstimulating visuals

STEP 3 — Lower One Point of Friction
Your friction-reduction change:

STEP 4 — Support Today's Capacity
Choose one:

- [ ] Declutter one surface
- [ ] Add a landing zone
- [ ] Create one visual anchor
- [ ] Reduce one routine to two steps
- [ ] Move a tool where you actually use it
- [ ] Sensory reset before starting

Try This Script

"My brain has changed. My systems get to change with it."

Try This: Capacity-Based Living Map

STEP 1 — Name Today's Capacity
- High
- Medium
- Low
- Bare-Minimum

Capacity notes: _______________________________________

STEP 2 — Choose What Fits
Pick 1-3:
- One essential task
- One micro-clean action
- One simplified routine
- One energy-preserving choice
- One request for help
- One task you'll intentionally NOT do today

STEP 3 — Adjust Expectations, Not Your Worth

"Today, a successful version of me looks like..."

STEP 4 — End-of-Day Compassion Check
Pick one:
- I adjusted instead of forcing.
- I honored my capacity.
- I redesigned instead of blaming.
- I supported my brain, not punished it.

Mini Tools + Resources

Mini Tool 1 — The Two-Step Routine
Reduce any routine to its core two steps. This keeps it functional even on low-capacity days.

Mini Tool 2 — The Anchor Object
Place one predictable cue in each room to ease transitions (tray, lamp, basket).

Mini Tool 3 — The One-Minute Reset
Clear one square foot of space. Stop there. Visual calm lowers cognitive load.

Mini Tool 4 — The Environ energy budget mental Pause
Before reacting or engaging dim lights, change rooms, sit, breathe.

Mini Tool 5 — The Communication Cue
"I'm at low capacity — can we keep things simple right now?"

Mini Tool 6 — The Energy Budget Check
Ask: "What truly deserves my energy today?"

Resource Highlight
Choose one friction point in your home or routine.

Redesign just that one point.
Notice how everything feels lighter.

8: Living the Plan, Integration in Real Life

There's a quiet turning point many women reach in this journey — a moment when the pieces begin to link together, not because everything is suddenly easy, but because it finally makes sense. You catch yourself recognizing patterns you once mislabeled as personal flaws. You notice hormonal shifts that used to feel random. Old coping strategies wobble and, instead of panicking, you think, *Right. This is part of it.* Understanding turns into clarity, and clarity becomes compassion. And compassion, more than anything, creates room to breathe.

But integration — actually living differently inside that new understanding — is its own kind of work. It isn't instantaneous, and it isn't linear. It's not a dramatic life makeover or a triumphant "before and after." Integration is a gentle recalibration of how you move through your days. It's lived-in change, the kind that develops quietly as your expectations shift and the tools you've learned begin to shape how you treat yourself.

This chapter isn't about perfection or mastery. It's about the deeply human process of adjusting to a brain that is still dynamic, still responsive, still sensitive — and still yours.

THE REAL SHAPE OF CHANGE

Most women imagine change as a straight trajectory forward — something you reach, maintain, and graduate from. Midlife doesn't work that way, especially not for an ADHD brain influenced by fluctuating hormones. Real change feels more like cycles than lines. Some days you feel steady, others chaotic. Some days you have clarity, others feel cloudy. Improvement and setbacks often sit side by side.

This isn't failure. It's physiology.

The most important part of integration is learning to interpret these shifts without shame. A day of fog doesn't erase the progress you've made. A surge of emotion doesn't mean you're falling apart. A low-capacity day doesn't erase a high-capacity week. Fluctuation is part of the landscape now, and integration means learning to move with it instead of assuming it means something about your character.

UNDERSTANDING YOUR NEW BASELINE

Many women hit a moment in midlife when they realize that trying to get "back to who I was" is no longer realistic — and more importantly, no longer necessary. You aren't meant to return to a previous version of yourself. You're meant to move forward with a brain that's updating its internal settings.

This is what a new baseline really means: not a lower standard, but a different one. Your energy, focus, emotional bandwidth, and capacity are shifting. That's not regression; it's recalibration. Integration means allowing yourself to operate according to the brain you have now rather than measuring yourself against who you were years ago. It means giving yourself permission to grow in a direction you didn't expect but absolutely can navigate.

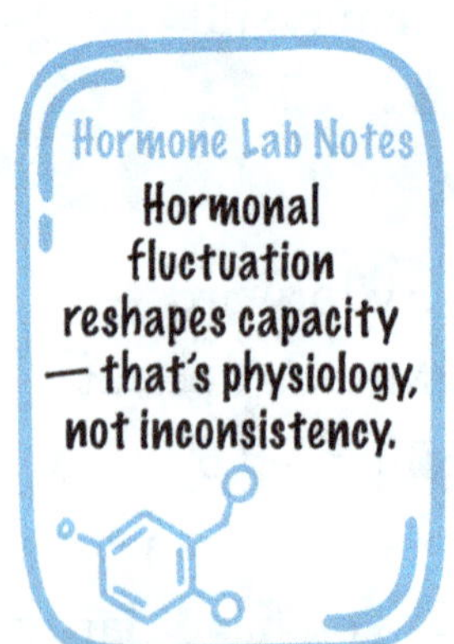

Midlife isn't the end of stability. It's the beginning of learning stability in a new form.

INTERNAL UNDERSTANDING AND EXTERNAL SUPPORT

Living the plan happens in two intertwined layers. Internal integration is the shift that happens inside your understanding of

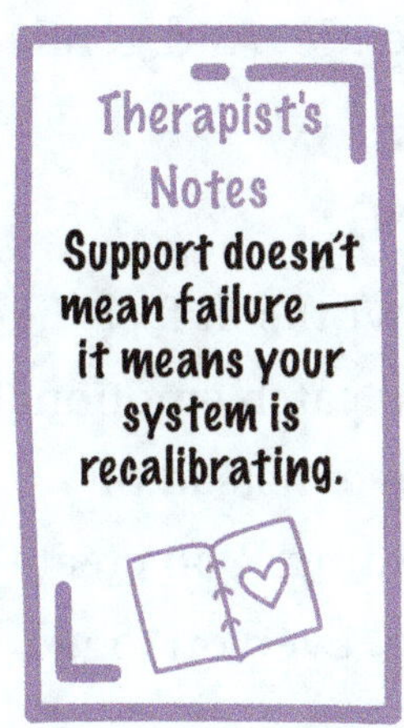

yourself — recognizing patterns, tracking capacity, acknowledging hormones, noticing emotional cues, and separating identity from biology. It's the internal story softening.

External integration is how that understanding shows up in your day-to-day life — the tools you use, the boundaries you set, the routines you simplify, the advocacy conversations you initiate, and the environments you design so you're not fighting friction with every task.

When these layers come together, something important changes. Internal understanding reduces shame; external support reduces strain. Together they create a stability that doesn't demand consistency but supports you even in inconsistency.

LETTING YOURSELF BE A WORK IN PROGRESS

Midlife integration often requires unlearning decades of habits: the instinct to push through exhaustion, the belief that rest must be earned, the pressure to remain constantly capable, the reflex to view support as failure. No chapter in any book can undo those patterns overnight. But awareness creates space — and space is where new patterns form.

Integration means giving yourself time to adjust. It means letting go of the idea that insight should immediately translate into

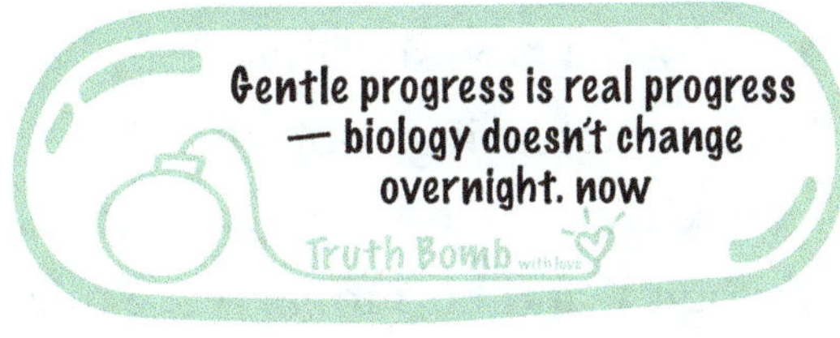

flawless behavior. It means accepting that you can understand your brain and still have days where everything feels harder. It means trusting that you're allowed to move slowly, to change your mind, to renegotiate expectations, and to rebuild routines without treating yourself like a renovation project. Progress here is gentle. And gentle is enough.

WHAT IT FEELS LIKE WHEN THINGS START WORKING

When integration settles in, it doesn't feel like fireworks. It feels like steadiness. You respond to yourself more kindly. You catch emotional surges before they spiral. Your routines feel supportive instead of burdensome. You notice your capacity before committing. You create fewer crises to recover from. You feel more grounded, even on foggy days.

Nothing is perfect — but fewer things feel impossible.

This shift isn't about symptoms disappearing; it's about how you relate to them. When your relationship with your brain becomes more compassionate, your resilience grows. You begin to experience your symptoms as signals rather than judgments. And that shift alone lessens their impact.

ADJUSTING EXPECTATIONS — YOURS AND EVERYONE ELSE'S

Midlife asks you to renegotiate expectations — both the ones you hold for yourself and the ones others still hold for you. This part can be uncomfortable, but it is essential.

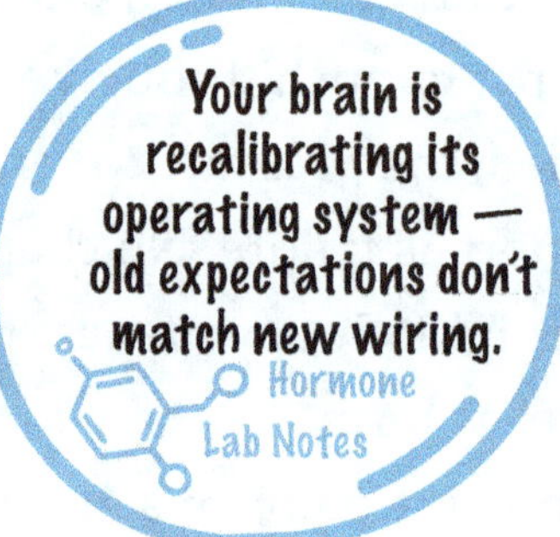

You are not being dramatic.
You are not "too sensitive."
You are not losing control.

You're learning how to function inside a brain undergoing a neurological and hormonal reorganization. Expecting yourself to operate as if nothing has changed will only create conflict. Integration requires adjusting expectations, so your daily life reflects your actual capacity, not outdated standards from a different season of your life.

Honest communication with yourself — and with others —becomes a form of emotional protection rather than confrontation. It creates room for support, and support creates room for steadiness.

THE LONG GAME: CHOOSING SUSTAINABILITY OVER PERFECTION

Sustainable systems will always outperform perfect ones, especially in a brain that runs on fluctuating internal chemistry. You're not building a flawless routine. You're building one you can return to, repair, and repeat — even on the days when motivation is low or emotions run high. The goal of this entire section isn't to make you more productive. It's to give you a life that doesn't drain you. A life that supports your brain instead of demanding that you constantly compensate for it. A life where you no longer confuse effort with worthiness.

You don't need to optimize everything.

You need to soften the parts that have been hard for a long time.

This is the heart of integration: choosing the rhythm that lets you function without self-punishment, without panic, and without pretending your brain hasn't changed.

PULLING PART II TOGETHER

Integration is where the medical, emotional, and practical finally converge. You now understand what's happening inside your brain. You know what supports you. You know the tools that make life smoother. You're learning to advocate, simplify, communicate, and stabilize. You're discovering how to trust yourself again — not the younger version of you, but the wiser one.

You're not fighting your brain anymore.

You're walking with it.

This chapter brings Part II to a close, and Part III opens with a deeper truth: once you understand yourself, you move through the world differently. You navigate differently. You respond differently. You begin to choose your well-being in ways that weren't available to you before.

You are not behind. You are not broken. You are becoming — steadily, gently, and in your own rhythm.

__What We Learned__

Key Insights

- Integration is not perfection — it is the quiet, steady process of living differently inside new understanding.
- Change in midlife ADHD is cyclical, not linear; fluctuation is physiology, not failure.
- Your "new baseline" is not lower — it is different, and adapting to it is a strength, not a loss.
- Internal integration softens shame; external integration reduces strain. Both are required for genuine stability.
- Progress here is gentle: noticing patterns, softening expectations, reducing crises, catching yourself with compassion.
- Adjusting expectations (yours and others') is not giving up — it is aligning your life with how your brain actually functions now.
- Sustainable systems will always outperform perfect ones. What matters is what you can return to, repair, and repeat.

What This Means for You

You're not meant to "go back" to who you were. You're meant to move forward with the brain you have — one that is updating its internal wiring and asking for new rhythms. Integration isn't about performing better; it's about living with less self-punishment. It's about steadiness replacing panic. It's about compassion replacing criticism. It's about designing a life that reduces friction instead of demanding consistency you cannot magically conjure.

Try This: The Integration Snapshot

A tool for noticing how your internal understanding and external supports are beginning to align.

STEP 1 — Where Am I Seeing Change Already?

Check any that apply:

- I catch patterns earlier
- I understand hormone-related shifts
- I adjust expectations sooner
- I design routines around capacity
- I ask for support sooner
- I notice emotional cues before spiraling
- I create fewer crises
- I speak to myself kindlier

STEP 2 — What Still Feels Wobbly?

(What area still slips, overwhelms you, or feels unpredictable?)

STEP 3 — Choose One Area to Integrate More Gently

(Examples: morning routine, work transitions, emotional cues, energy dips, planning, communication.)

My focus: ____

STEP 4 — Set a Gentle Integration Cue

Pick one or write your own:

- "Slow is still forward."
- "Fluctuation is not failure."
- "I'm learning a new rhythm."
- "My brain is changing — my expectations can too."

My cue: ____

Capacity Mapping — What's My Real Range Right Now?

A visual tool for understanding your usable capacity on different types of days.

STEP 1 — Identify Your Three Most Common Capacity States

Check any that fit you:

- High capacity days — clarity, flow, easier transitions
- Medium capacity days — functional but slower, need pacing
- Low capacity days — foggy, overstimulated, overwhelmed

STEP 2 — What Does Each State Look Like for You?

Fill in examples:

High capacity:

- ____
- ____

Medium capacity:

- ____
- ____

Low capacity:

- ____
- ____

STEP 3 — What Helps Each State?

List 2-3 supports for each:

High capacity supports:

- Structure
- Hard tasks first
- Creative work
- Other:

Medium capacity supports:

- Breaks
- Simple routines
- Lower output
- Other:

Low capacity supports:

- Sensory reset
- One tiny task
- Hydration + protein
- Other:

STEP 4 — One Thing You'll Stop Expecting From Low-Capacity You

The Baseline Reset Tool

A guided way to identify what your *new normal* actually feels like.

STEP 1 — What Does a "Good Enough" Day Look Like Now?
(Name 2-4 elements, not tasks.)

STEP 2 — What Are My Signals That Capacity Is Dropping?
Check any that match you:

- Irritability
- Emotional surges
- Brain fog
- Motor slow-down
- Feeling "far away"
- Lose words / trouble thinking
- Everything feels heavier
- Noise becomes intolerable
- Trouble initiating simple tasks

Other: ____

STEP 3 — What Helps Me Stabilize?
(Choose 2-3 realistic supports.)

- A sensory reset
- A 10-minute pause
- Light + hydration
- Protein
- Simplifying plans
- Asking for clarity
- A slower pace
- A small reset (one room, one task)

My stabilizers: ____

STEP 4 — One Expectation I'm Releasing

PUTTING IT INTO PRACTICE

<u>**Reflection + Integration**</u>

Reflection Prompts

1. What expectations of my "old self" am I unconsciously trying to meet?
2. What feels different now that I understand the biology behind my symptoms?
3. Where am I still interpreting physiology as personal failure?
4. What part of my routine or environment has become noticeably easier?
5. How can I communicate my shifting capacity with honesty instead of apology?

Journaling Space

Helpful Insight

> "Integration isn't about doing everything right —
> it's about relating to yourself differently."

<u>Mini Tools + Resources</u>

Mini Tool 1 — The Two-Minute Orientation#
Before starting anything, pause and ask:
"What version of me showed up today?"
Align tasks accordingly.

Mini Tool 2 — The Baseline Reminder
Keep a note somewhere visible:
"My worth is not measured by my capacity."

Mini Tool 3 — The Gentle Re-Entry
After a foggy day, return with the smallest possible anchor: one load of laundry, one email, one room reset, one step.

Mini Tool 4 — The Communication Softener
Script:
"My brain is running low bandwidth today. I'm present — just slower."

Mini Tool 5 — The Expectation Reset
Lower one expectation today. Not because you can't — but because you shouldn't have to push that hard anymore.

Mini Tool 6 — The Compassion Loop
When you slip into old patterns, pause and say:
"This is part of learning. Nothing has gone wrong."

Resource Highlight
Create an "Integration Map" in your Notes app with:
- Your capacity signals
- Your stabilizers
- Your communication cue
- Your expectation reset

Use it as a living reference — a gentle guide rather than a strict plan.

Part III: Practical Tools That Work

There comes a point in every woman's ADHD–menopause journey when understanding the science is no longer enough. You can know *exactly* why your brain feels unpredictable, why your emotions spike, why your meds fluctuate, why your memory slips — and still find yourself standing in the kitchen thinking, "Okay, but what do I actually do right now?"

Part III is where we answer that. This is the section where all the insight and self-compassion you've built so far become usable. Not rigid systems. Not productivity hacks that require perfect hormone balance or unbroken focus. Not color-coded routines that collapse the moment life gets messy.

The tools in this section are designed for real women, living real lives, with real fluctuations. They're flexible. They're forgiving. They're grounded in neuroscience and shaped by lived experience. And they're meant to support you on the days when your brain works beautifully — and the days when it absolutely does not. Think of these tools the way you think of grabbing a sweater on a cold day. You don't overhaul your entire wardrobe or remodel the house with a new heating system. You just use what helps in the moment, because a small adjustment is all that is needed. These tools work the same way — they meet you where you are, not where you wish you were.

In the chapters ahead, you'll find systems that make your life lighter, not heavier. Tools that help you initiate tasks, manage energy, calm your nervous system, create structure without suffocation, and rebuild confidence in your own capacity. Some of them you'll use every day. Some you'll reach for only when things wobble. All of them are here to give you a way forward when your brain feels unpredictable.

You've done the understanding. You've done the reframing.

You've done the emotional work. Now we build the "how."

9: Fractal Tools for Real Life

There's a moment that happens for almost every woman trying to get through midlife with ADHD. You sit down with the best intentions — to plan the day, start the task, finally get a handle on things — and your brain simply… refuses. Not in a dramatic, meltdown kind of way. More like a low battery signal you didn't see coming. And no matter what system you try to use, it feels too big or too complicated for the capacity you actually have.

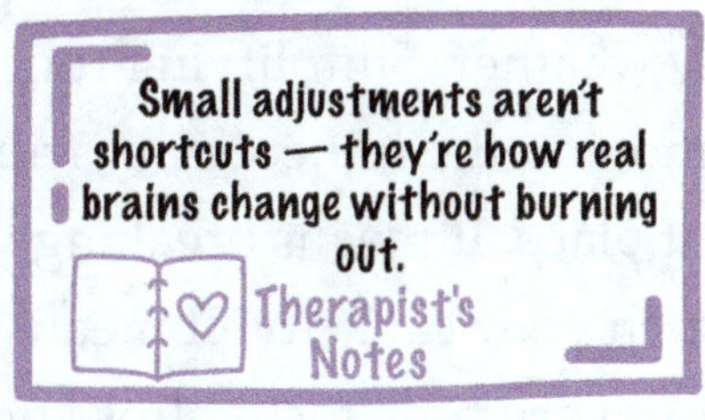

This chapter is about the tools made for *that* moment.

Tools that flex with your fluctuating attention.

Tools that shrink when your bandwidth shrinks.

Tools that expand when you feel capable.

Tools that don't punish you for being human.

I call them fractal tools — systems that work at every size. They function when you have a full hour of focus or when you have five wobbly minutes. They scale up and down instantly. They don't collapse when your hormones shift or your dopamine dips. And they don't ask you to be a version of yourself you can't reliably access.

Fractal tools are the opposite of perfectionism. They're the opposite of shame.

They're the opposite of "I should be doing more."

They're designed for midlife ADHD brains — brains that need flexible scaffolding, not rigid architecture.

SIMPLIFYING ROUTINES SO THEY CAN SURVIVE REAL LIFE

Most of us spent years trying to build routines that only worked under perfect conditions — the right amount of sleep, the right

"

emotional energy, the right environment, the right motivation. If any piece was missing, the whole system crumbled.

Midlife demands something different: systems that can function in any weather. Simplifying routines doesn't mean doing less; it means removing the unnecessary friction that keeps you from starting in the first place. It means breaking your day into pieces small enough to match your capacity. It means resisting the urge to "fix your whole life" every time focus slips and instead choosing the smallest next thing that keeps you moving forward. A fractal routine works on good days *and* bad days. On good days it expands naturally — you do a little more, move a little faster, feel a little clearer. On hard days it shrinks and still counts. This is how routines survive hormonal instability. This is how women stay functional without burning out. It's not about discipline. It's about design.

HOW TO SUPPORT YOUR BRAIN IN THE MOMENT—WHAT ACTUALLY HELPS

Midlife ADHD brains need fuel — and not in the "optimize your productivity" sense. They need micro-supports throughout the day that stabilize attention, calm internal noise, and keep tasks from feeling impossible. These aren't hacks in the gimmicky sense; they're physiological nudges that help your brain shift gears.

Focus fuel is anything that gives your brain the internal conditions it needs to initiate a task: hydration, protein, a body movement reset, changing locations, sensory stimulation, light, novelty, cold exposure, warmth, music, caffeine at the right moment. These aren't random tricks — they're ways of engaging the systems that regulate arousal and attention.

The key is this: you don't need the same thing every day.

Your brain's needs shift with hormones, sleep, stress, and emotion.

Some days your brain wants stimulation.

Some days it wants calm.

Some days it wants movement.

Some days it wants predictability.

Fractal tools let you respond quickly rather than guessing or blaming yourself. They let you ask, "What version of fuel does my brain need today?" instead of "What is wrong with me?"

When you learn how to give your brain the right conditions instead of coercing it, initiation gets easier, overwhelm decreases, and the day becomes more doable.

STRUCTURE WITHOUT RIGIDITY

Midlife teaches women something most systems never prepare them for: structure doesn't have to mean constraint. So many ADHD women associate structure with shame — rules they couldn't follow, planners they abandoned, routines that collapsed, expectations that felt suffocating. But structure is not the enemy. *Rigidity* is.

Structure with softness — structure that bends, shrinks, expands, and forgives — is what supports ADHD brains. It's a framework that holds you without trapping you. It's the difference between having a map and being told the exact route you *must* take.

+ Rigid systems break the moment your capacity fluctuates.
+ Flexible systems adapt to your capacity automatically

This kind of structure offers guardrails, not walls. It gives you a sense of direction without demanding consistency you can't reliably maintain. It frees you from decision fatigue without stealing your autonomy. Flexible structure is how you stay grounded when hormones steal predictability.

It's how you build a life that fits your brain — not a life you spend all your energy trying to keep up with.

Fractal tools are not shortcuts. They're not productivity hacks. They're not about squeezing more out of yourself or proving anything to anyone.

They're about building a life that adjusts to you instead of forcing you to adjust to it. These tools give you a way to navigate real days — the messy ones, the scattered ones, the emotionally heavy ones, the surprising bursts of clarity. They let you show up for yourself with compassion instead of punishment, flexibility instead of

frustration. Most importantly, they make room for the truth you've been learning throughout this book:

Your brain isn't unreliable — your *systems* were. Now you're building systems that can actually hold the woman you are today.

In the next chapter, we'll take these fractal tools and apply them to your day-to-day life — routines, environments, relationships, and the practical adjustments that make living with midlife ADHD feel sustainable instead of overwhelming.

Building a life that fits today — not the one you think you "should" carry.

PUTTING IT INTO PRACTICE

What We Learned

Key Insights

- Midlife ADHD brains need tools that adjust to fluctuating capacity — not systems that collapse the moment conditions shift.
- Fractal tools work at every size: they expand on high-capacity days and shrink on low-capacity days without losing function.
- Simplifying routines reduces friction, making it easier to start tasks and maintain momentum even during hormonal instability.
- Your brain needs "focus fuel" throughout the day — micro-supports like movement, hydration, protein, novelty, light, and sensory resets help regulate attention.
- Structure is not the enemy — rigidity is. Soft, flexible structure supports ADHD brains far better than strict systems.
- Fractal design allows you to take the smallest possible next step instead of trying to "fix your whole life."
- You're not unreliable — your systems were. Now you're building structure that adapts to your real brain in real life.

What This Means for You

You don't need more discipline. You don't need more motivation. You don't need a color-coded system that requires perfect conditions to work. You need routines, tools, and supports that meet you where your brain is today — not where it was last year or where other people think it should be. Fractal tools give you a way to scale your life up or down without shame or collapse. They let you stay functional on hard days and thrive on easier days. This chapter is your invitation to stop forcing yourself into rigid systems and start building ones that flex with you.

Try This: The Fractal Task Shrinker

What This Tool Does

Helps you shrink any task into versions that match your capacity — high, medium, low, or bare-minimum — so the task stays doable on any kind of day.

1. Pick One Task

(Example: laundry, email, kitchen cleaning, work project.)

2. Write the Four Versions (Use the mini examples to guide you.)

High-Capacity Version
("Do all laundry, fold, put away.)

Standard Version
("Wash full load start to finish)

Small Version
(Wash one load, skip folding.)

Bare-Minimum Version
(Gather clothes in one basket.)

3. What Capacity Do You Have Today?

- High
- Medium
- Low
- Bare-Minimum

Today I'll do:

____

4. Add One Piece of Focus Fuel (choose one quick support)

- Water
- Protein
- Movement
- Sensory reset
- Light
- Change rooms
- Music

My pick:

____

5. Start With the Version That Fits Today

Every version is valid. Every version counts.

Reflection + Integration

Reflection Prompts

1. What routine or task collapses most often when my capacity drops?
2. What is one area of my life where I need softer, more flexible structure? What focus fuel does my brain respond to most reliably?
3. How would my days change if I stopped expecting the "high capacity" version of myself to show up every day?

Journaling Space

Helpful Insight

> "You don't need a bigger version of yourself —
> you need smaller versions of your tasks."

Mini Tools + Resources

Mini Tool 1 — The Five-Minute Bridge

If a task feels impossible, set a timer for five minutes. Do only what fits inside that window. Stopping after five minutes is allowed.

Mini Tool 2 — The Two-Step Routine

Every routine has a "core two steps." Identify them so the routine never fully collapses. (Example: Morning = brush teeth + get dressed. Evening = dishes in sink + turn off lights.)

Mini Tool 3 — The Friction Check

Ask: "What tiny piece of friction is making this harder?" Remove just that one thing — not the whole problem.

Mini Tool 4 — The Tiny Reset

Shift one small sensory input: open a window, adjust lighting, stretch for 10 seconds, change rooms, drink water. Small resets = big regulation.

Mini Tool 5 — The Micro-List

Write a list of *three* things only. When you finish those, you're done. Everything else is optional.

Mini Tool 6 — The One-Object Tidy

Put away one object. Just one. If momentum shows up, great. If not, the one object still counts.

Resource Highlight

Choose one routine in your life (morning, kitchen reset, work start, end-of-day). Use the Fractal Task Shrinker to build the four versions now — so you're never starting from zero on low-capacity days.

10: Reality Based Solutions

There's a moment in midlife when you look at your day — the calendar, the inbox, the to-do list that multiplies when you look away for five minutes — and you realize your hormones and your responsibilities have once again teamed up against you. Your brain feels foggy, your focus is slippery, your emotions are thin-skinned, and somehow the simplest things now feel like you're wading through wet cement. And yet the world keeps expecting you to function.

Reality-based solutions are what keep women afloat during this phase — not because they make everything easy, but because they make things *possible*. These aren't idealized systems pulled from a productivity blog. They're the kinds of strategies women discover when they're living inside the conflict of "I have to get things done" and "My brain is shutting down."

This chapter is about what actually helps on those days — the days when your hormones betray you, your to-do list mocks you, and your brain feels inconsistent in ways that are both predictable and wildly unfair. It's about learning to work with the brain you have in the moment, not the brain you wish you still had.

WHEN YOUR HORMONES AND YOUR TO-DO LIST BETRAY YOU

There will be days when the simplest task feels like climbing a cliff in the wrong shoes. Days when your brain won't transition between tasks. Days when emotions sit closer to the surface. Days when your medication does nothing or does too much. Days when you can feel your executive function slipping through your fingers like loose change.

Most women interpret these moments as failure.

"They shouldn't be this hard."

"Why can't I just do it?"

"What is wrong with me today?"

But nothing is wrong with you.

This is what hormonal volatility feels like in an ADHD brain — inconsistent energy, fluctuating motivation, unpredictable emotional bandwidth, and a to-do list that doesn't care.

Reality-based solutions begin with accepting that some days require a different operating system. It's not resignation — it's recognition. When you understand that your capacity shifts hour to hour, you stop expecting yourself to function as if every day is the same. You start adjusting your approach instead of blaming yourself for your biology. There is enormous freedom in that shift.

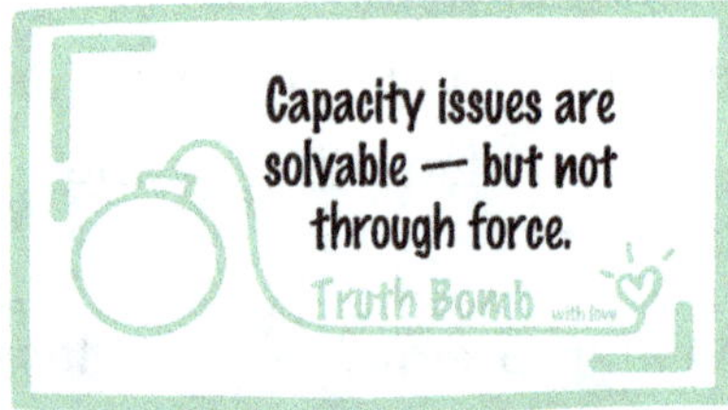

Oh… this isn't a character flaw. This is a capacity issue.

And capacity issues are solvable — but not through force. Through strategy

REAL-WORLD STRATEGIES FOR WORK, RELATIONSHIPS, AND SELF-CARE

Work, relationships, and self-care are the areas where ADHD and menopause create the most friction — not because you're less capable, but because the demands in these areas rarely shrink when your brain does. Midlife is often the moment women are asked to juggle the most while having the least buffer to do it.

Reality-based strategies acknowledge that truth.

They're built on the understanding that your brain has different versions of itself.

They make room for fluctuation instead of pretending it shouldn't exist.

At work, this looks like choosing the path of least resistance on low-capacity days — the smaller task, the shorter email, the five-minute version instead of the hour-long ideal. It looks like building tiny transitions into your day, so your brain doesn't have to jump abruptly from one mode to another. It looks like understanding that your best work doesn't come from white knuckling through a hormone dip, but from working with your brain's natural rhythms whenever possible.

In relationships, reality-based solutions mean communicating your capacity with honesty instead of apology. It means recognizing when irritability is a hormone talking rather than a relationship emergency. It means stepping away when your nervous system is overloaded, not as avoidance, but as preservation. It means asking for clarity, slowing down conversations, and letting your partner know, "I'm not checked out — my brain just needs a second to catch up."

And in self-care — the kind that actually matters — it means redefining what counts. Some days care looks like a workout. Some days it looks like drinking a glass of water and going to bed earlier. Some days it looks like a good cry. Some days it looks like doing the bare minimum with your whole heart and calling it a win.

Self-care is not a ritual. Self-care is responsiveness — meeting your brain's needs in real time, without judgment.

TOOLS THAT ACTUALLY FIT THE ADHD + MENOPAUSE BRAIN

Most tools fail ADHD women because they're designed for brains that don't fluctuate. They assume consistent energy, predictable focus, stable emotions, and a reliable sense of motivation. Midlife blows a hole through those assumptions.

The tools that actually work here are the ones that shrink and expand with you. Tools that understand inconsistency isn't a flaw — it's a feature of your neurobiology. Tools that give you what you need without requiring a version of yourself you can't summon on command.

These tools feel different because they're built differently. They don't demand linear effort. They don't shame you for having limits. They don't fall apart when you're overstimulated, under-slept, emotionally raw, or hormonally scrambled. They are tools that offer guidance without pressure, structure without rigidity, direction without demand. They are the tools that let you move gently through your day while still moving at all. When a tool fits the ADHD + menopause brain, you feel it immediately.

Your shoulders drop.

Your breath steadies.

Something inside you unclenches.

The task doesn't become easy — it becomes *possible*.

And for many women, possible is enough. Possible is everything.

PULLING IT ALL TOGETHER

Reality-based solutions don't ask you to be superhuman. They don't require discipline you can't maintain or focus you don't have. They let you build a life that flexes with your capacity, not against it. They help you stay functional during hormone storms, emotional dips, and the unpredictable rhythms of a brain that has been through decades of over functioning

This chapter is your reminder that sustainable living isn't about mastering your brain — it's about partnering with it. It's learning to listen to the early signals, respond without shame, and adjust without fear. It's honoring the woman you are right now instead of chasing the woman you think you should be.

In the next chapter, we'll take these reality-based strategies and weave them into the environments, relationships, and rhythms that shape your everyday life — so the support around you matches the support inside you.

<u>What We Learned</u>

Key Insights
- Midlife ADHD brains operate with shifting capacity — energy, focus, motivation, and emotional bandwidth change from hour to hour, not day to day.
- Hormonal volatility collides with daily responsibilities, making "simple tasks" feel impossible during dips.
- Reality-based solutions remove shame by matching tasks to your *actual* brain in the moment, not the "best case scenario" version of yourself.
- Work, relationships, and self-care all become easier when you stop forcing consistency and start adjusting your approach based on capacity.
- Self-care is not a ritual — it's responsiveness. It's giving your brain what it needs today, not what worked last week.
- Tools that fit midlife ADHD are flexible, forgiving, and scalable. They don't collapse when your hormones do.
- Possible is enough. Possible is everything.

What This Means for You

You don't have to battle your brain every time your capacity dips. You don't have to push through low-focus days with the same expectations you have on your best days. Reality-based solutions let you adapt so you can function without burning out. When you stop treating fluctuations as failures, you start seeing your symptoms as signals — information that helps you plan smarter, gentler, and with far more self-respect. This chapter is an invitation to build a daily life that responds to who you are now, not who you were ten years ago.

PUTTING IT INTO PRACTICE

Try This: The Reality-Based Daily Plan
Purpose: To help you plan your day according to your *real* capacity — not pressure, perfectionism, or guilt. This tool keeps your workload doable even when your brain feels unstable, foggy, or overloaded.

1. What's My Capacity Today? (Choose the one that feels most accurate right now.)
 - High — I feel clear, steady, and capable
 - Medium — I can do things, but need pacing
 - Low — only small, simple steps are doable
 - Bare-Minimum — I need relief-focused support

2. What Absolutely Matters Today? (1–3 items max. "Enough" is the goal.)

3. Right-Size Today's Tasks Take one task and match it to today's capacity.
Task:
 - High version:
 - Medium version:
 - Low version:
 - Bare-minimum version:

4. Support My Brain (Pick at least one)
 - Hydration
 - Bright light
 - Change environment
 - Pause before responding
 - Take a sensory reset (cold/warm/quiet)
 - Protein
 - Small movement break
 - Ask for clarity
 - Set a micro-timer

5. One Gentle Cue for the Day
 - "Capacity is not character."
 - "Small moves keep me afloat."
 - "Low-capacity days still count."
 - "My brain is shifting — not failing."

<u>Reflection + Integration</u>

Reflection Prompts
1. Where do I blame myself for capacity changes that are hormonal or neurological?
2. What area of my life (work, home, relationships) needs more reality-based expectations?
3. When I look back, what's one moment where responding gently to my capacity helped me?
4. What signs tell me that my capacity is dropping before I fully crash?

Journaling Space

Helpful Insight
"You are not inconsistent — your capacity shifts.
Your strategies are allowed to shift too."

Mini Tools + Resources

Mini Tool 1 — The Capacity Check
Ask: "Is this a high, medium, low, or bare-minimum moment?"
Match your tasks to the answer.

Mini Tool 2 — The Tiny Transition
Before switching tasks, pause for 10 seconds. Stand, stretch,
breathe, or change your sensory input. Soft transitions protect
your brain.

Mini Tool 3 — The Half-Step Strategy
If a task feels too big, ask: "What is half of this?" Do only that.
Half still counts.

Mini Tool 4 — Relationship Capacity Cue
Say: "My brain is overloaded. I need a minute, not distance."
This protects connection without overextending yourself.

Mini Tool 5 — Self-Care Redefined
Pick one of these and let it be enough today:
- Water
- Protein
- Rest
- Cry
- Step outside
- One-room reset

Resource Highlight

Try using the Reality-Based Daily Plan for one week. Notice how your
stress lowers when tasks match capacity instead of willpower

There's a moment in midlife when you catch yourself in the middle of something utterly ridiculous — crying because you can't find the salad tongs, laughing in the middle of an argument, standing in the pantry with no idea why you're there — and you wonder how a fully grown adult can feel this disoriented by her own brain. What you don't see in that moment is the millions of women living the same experience, often silently, often assuming they're the only ones unraveling at the seams. But you're not unraveling. You're human in a phase of life that bends your neurological wiring and emotional thresholds in ways no one prepared you for. What softens this stage — what truly anchors you — is connection, humor, and the kind of gentle guidance that helps you make sense of your experience without judging it.

TURNING CHAOS INTO CONNECTION

One of the most healing experiences for women in midlife is realizing that the chaos they've been quietly ashamed of is, in fact, common. ADHD and hormonal change create a kind of mental static that can make your thoughts unpredictable, your emotions louder, and your attention fickle. But when you share these moments with someone who genuinely understands — someone who doesn't blink when you say you found your keys in the freezer or cried at a commercial — the shame dissolves.

What once felt like a personal failure becomes a point of connection. The story you were embarrassed to tell becomes the exact moment someone else exhales in relief because they thought they were the only one. Chaos becomes context, and context becomes comfort. Empathy doesn't eliminate difficulty, but it changes the entire emotional texture. You stop seeing your experience as evidence that something is wrong with you and start seeing it as a predictable part of a transition that many women navigate.

USING HUMOR AS RESILIENCE

Humor is not a distraction from the hard parts — it's a release valve for your nervous system. Midlife ADHD produces moments that are genuinely absurd, and sometimes the only honest response is to laugh. You lose your train of thought mid-sentence and pivot into an entirely different story. You tear up because someone said "good morning" in a tone that hit you sideways. You forget the word for a common object and end up describing it in a way that makes complete sense to only you.

Humor doesn't minimize the real frustrations of this phase; it opens a little space around them so you can breathe. It helps you recover from moments that would otherwise feel too heavy or too sharp. It

reminds you that you're dealing with a brain that's doing its best inside unpredictable wiring, and sometimes its best is unintentionally hilarious. Finding humor in these moments isn't avoidance — it's resilience. It's how you keep going without collapsing under the weight of perfection or pressure.

NORMALIZING THE STRUGGLE AND CELEBRATING ADAPTABILITY

There is nothing pathological about finding this stage difficult. Your brain is renegotiating its relationship with hormones that have quietly stabilized your emotional world, your focus, and your stress tolerance for decades. Of course, things feel different now. Of course, some days feel impossible, and other days feel mysteriously easy. Struggle is normal here, not because you're doing something wrong, but because your internal systems are in motion.

What deserves far more attention than the difficulty is your adaptability. You pivot constantly — adjusting your expectations, shifting your strategies, inventing workarounds, learning to function in a body and brain that rarely feel the same two days in a row. That isn't inconsistency. It's intelligence. It's resilience. It's the flexibility that has carried you through responsibilities, relationships, and life transitions long before you had a name for the way your brain works.

Adaptability becomes even more powerful when you stop expecting yourself to be steady in a life stage defined by fluctuation. When you stop interpreting inconsistency as a character flaw, you make space for compassion. You make space for the truth that some days

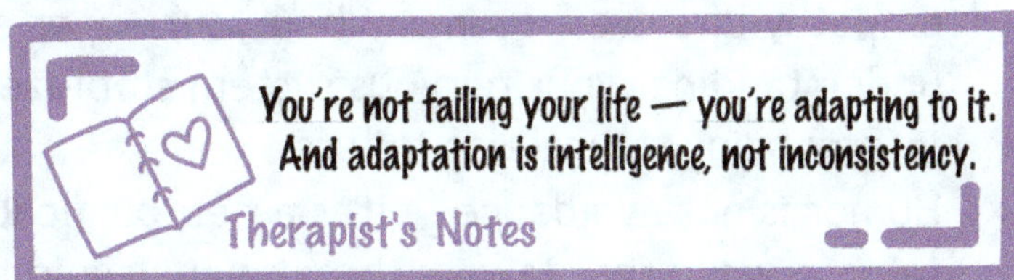

require a lighter touch, and some days you will surprise yourself with clarity. Letting your capacity guide your choices instead of fighting yourself is not giving up; it's honoring the real conditions of your life.

PULLING IT ALL TOGETHER

Empathy gives you perspective, humor gives you breathing room, and guidance gives you direction — not the kind that demands perfection but the kind that helps you move through the world with more steadiness and less self-blame. These elements don't replace therapy or medication or the practical tools you've learned; they make every other strategy sustainable. They remind you that your experience is shared, that your challenges make sense, and that you have agency even in the most unpredictable moments.

You have spent a lifetime adapting, problem-solving, and persisting in environments that weren't designed with your brain in mind. Now, you get to use that same adaptability with more clarity, more compassion, and a much deeper understanding of what's happening inside you. Your struggle is real — and so is your strength. As you move into the next chapters of your life, let your humor, your empathy, and your hard-won wisdom lead the way. You're not doing this perfectly. You're doing it bravely. And that is more than enough.

PUTTING IT INTO PRACTICE

What We Learned

Key Insights
- Midlife ADHD creates emotional, cognitive, and sensory unpredictability that can feel disorienting — but it is shared by millions of women.
- Empathy dissolves shame. When your experience is met with understanding, your nervous system stabilizes and you stop internalizing struggle as failure.
- Humor is not avoidance — it is a neurologically protective release valve that lowers threat signals and helps you recover from overwhelm.
- Connection transforms chaos into context. What once felt embarrassing becomes common when shared with someone who understands.
- Adaptability — not consistency — is the real skill of midlife. Your ability to pivot, adjust, and keep going is not a flaw; it's resilience.
- Inconsistency is not a character issue. It's a predictable by-product of hormonal fluctuation layered onto a neurodivergent brain.
- Empathy, humor, and gentle guidance make every other tool (CBT, medication support, routines, focus strategies) more effective and sustainable.

What This Means for You

You are not overreacting, unraveling, or losing your grip — you are navigating one of the most neurologically complex phases of your life. Nothing about your experience is strange or shameful. The moments you think are "ridiculous" or "too much" are the same moments other women whisper "me too." Humor helps you let go. Empathy gives you a soft landing. Guidance gives you direction without pressure. You deserve support that sees your humanity as clearly as your symptoms.

PUTTING IT INTO PRACTICE

<u>Try This: The "Name It, Laugh a Little, Normalize It"</u>

Purpose: To help you normalize your experience, soften shame, and use humor + empathy to regulate your nervous system instead of spiraling.

1. Name the Moment: What happened that felt chaotic, emotional, or "I can't believe this is my life"?

2. What Was the Emotion Underneath? Choose all that apply

- Frustrated
- Hurt
- Embarrassed
- Overwhelmed
- Confused
- Jittery
- Teary
- Irritated
- Tender

3. Add a Dash of Humor (If You Can)
   Pick one:

- "Of course this happened today.
- "My brain has left the chat."
- "This is ridiculous — and also... relatable."
- "This is peak midlife ADHD."
- Write your own:

4. Normalize It

Choose one that feels grounding:

- "This makes sense for what my brain is doing right now."
- "Nothing is wrong with me — my wiring is shifting."
- "Other women experience this every single day."
- "This is common. Not catastrophic."

5. What Support Would Help Right Now?

- Tell someone who understands
- Step away for a moment
- Drink water
- Ask for clarity in a conversation
- Something else:
- Cry (valid)
- Deep breath + reset
- Lower today's expectations
- Rest my eyes

Gentle Cue "This moment doesn't define me. It's just a moment — and I'm allowed to meet it with softness."

Reflection + Integration

Reflection Prompts

1. What recent moment felt chaotic or surprising — and what made sense about it when you zoomed out?

2. Where do I need more empathy (from myself or others) in this stage of life?

3. What makes me laugh about my midlife ADHD experience?

4. Who in my life can hold my messy moments with gentleness and humor?

Journaling Space

Helpful Insight

"You're not doing this perfectly —
you're doing it bravely. And brave is enough."

PUTTING IT INTO PRACTICE

<u>Mini Tools + Resources</u>

Mini Tool 1 — The Humor Interrupt
One light, silly line to break the shame spiral:
"My brain is buffering... please wait."

Mini Tool 2 — The Empathy Anchor
Place a hand on your chest and say:
"This is human. This is normal. This is okay."

Mini Tool 3 — The Permission Slip
Give yourself permission for one thing today:
rest • a pause • fewer expectations • a do-over • a lighter load.
Write yours:

Mini Tool 4 — The Emotional Weather Report
Name the moment like weather:
"Today is foggy with a 70% chance of random tears."
It helps you detach from self-blame.

Mini Tool 5 — Tell Someone Who Gets It
Send a text to a friend who understands:
"You will not believe what my brain just did..."
Connection reduces cortisol.

Resource Highlight
Create a tiny "humor + empathy list" in your Notes app — one line
to make you laugh, one line to reassure you, one line to ground
you. Use it on high-emotion day

.

Epilogue

YOU MADE IT HERE — AND THAT MATTERS

If you're holding this book in your hands, it means you've walked through a landscape most women were never warned about. You've lived inside a brain that shifts without permission, inside a body that keeps renegotiating its rules, and inside a culture that expects steadiness from women even as their biology becomes anything but steady.

And still, you're here.

Still curious.

Still hopeful.

Still reaching for understanding.

That says more about your strength than you probably allow yourself to believe.

Nothing about this journey has been simple. ADHD was already a winding path; menopause added a few extra switchbacks, some surprising plot twists, and the occasional emotional cliff. But you kept going. You kept asking questions. You kept listening to your own experience — even when it felt confusing, contradictory, or downright unfair.

If there is one truth to take with you, let it be this:

Your brain is not failing you.

It is changing — and you are learning to change with it.

The strategies, tools, and workbook exercises you've gathered here were never meant to turn you into someone else. They were designed to help you live more gently inside the self you already are — the one who has always adapted, always pushed through, always carried more than anyone realized. You have earned more compassion than you've ever given yourself. You deserve a future built on that compassion, not criticism.

As you move forward, there will still be days that feel foggy or loud or unexpectedly emotional. There will be days that surprise you with clarity and ease. There will be days that fall somewhere in between. None of these days define you. They are simply the rhythm of a brain and body in motion.

What defines you is how you meet yourself inside that rhythm.

If you remember nothing else, remember this:

You are capable.

You are resilient.

You are not alone.

Every woman who picks up this book is walking her own version of this path — different details, same terrain. Somewhere out there is another woman crying over the wrong brand of paper towels or laughing at the chaos in her own kitchen, wondering if anyone else feels this way. You've just spent an entire book learning that they do.

Carry that connection with you. Carry the humor. Carry the guidance.
Carry the permission to be fully human in a phase of life that demands honesty, grace, and flexibility.

Your story is still unfolding — with more insight, more compassion, and more support than you had before. And now, as you step into whatever comes next, you do so with a deeper understanding of yourself than at any point in your life.

You are doing the best you can with a brain that has been through a lot.

And the best you can is more than enough.

A Final Reflection

There will be days when your mind feels focused and sure, and days when it wanders in a dozen directions, refusing to settle. Some mornings will arrive with clarity, and others will ask you to navigate fog thick enough to feel like weather inside your bones.

But none of it means you're failing.
It means you're human — and it means you're still here, moving through a life that has asked more of you than most people will ever understand.

You have survived every season that tried to undo you — every hormone storm, every impossible morning, every quiet heartbreak, every loud moment you thought you couldn't carry, every moment you were sure would break you but didn't. Every challenge that was meant to take you down has already been outlived.

Meet yourself with the same strength you've already proven through grit and grace. Let yourself be a work in progress — allowed to grow, rebuild, rest, rise, fall, try again, and become whoever you need to be next.

And as you move forward, remember this:

You are not defined by the hard days.
You are defined by the fact that you have risen through all of them — and you're still rising now.
You are not done.
You are becoming.

If you've made it to this page, I'm genuinely grateful you stayed with me — through the science, the stories, the messy truths, the humor, and the deeply human parts of this journey. I wrote this book the same way I sit with clients in my office: with honesty, warmth, curiosity, and absolutely no judgment. Because midlife ADHD isn't something anyone should navigate alone or silently.

There was a morning — one of those nothing-special days — when I opened my refrigerator and found my keys sitting on the shelf. I had zero memory of putting them there. I just stood there staring, thinking, *"Really? After everything I know. After everything I teach. This is still my brain?"*

And the truth was: yes.
It was still my brain.

A brain shifting with hormones, shifting with life, shifting with seasons I didn't choose — and still doing its best to show up. That moment didn't undo me. It clarified me.

I kept meeting women who thought they were falling apart — women apologizing for symptoms that had a biological explanation, women convinced they were the only ones struggling, women carrying invisible loads with grit and grace that no one ever acknowledged. Women who believed they were the problem, when in reality their brains and bodies were simply changing — and no one had given them a map.

If you recognized yourself anywhere in these pages, I want you to hear this as clearly as I can say it:
Nothing about your experience is a flaw.
Nothing about your struggle is a failure.
Nothing about your harder days makes you less capable, less worthy, or less whole.

You have survived every season that tried to undo you — every hormone storm, every impossible morning, every quiet heartbreak, every loud moment you thought you couldn't carry, every transition you never asked for but lived through anyway. Your track record for getting through hard things is 100%.

You've adapted in a thousand ways across your life — often quietly, often without support, often without language for what you were moving through. And you're still adapting now, but with more understanding, more compassion, and more truth than you had before.

If there is one thing I hope you carry with you, it's this:

Be on your own side.

Talk to yourself the way you would talk to someone you love. Give yourself room to rest, room to grow, room to be human. Give yourself credit for how much you've carried — because it's a lot.

Thank you for letting me walk beside you in these pages. Thank you for trusting me with your questions, your fears, your humor, and your hope — even if we never sat in the same room. It has been an honor to share this space with you.

You're not behind.

You're not breaking.

You're becoming — and you're doing it with more strength and courage than you realize.

— **Kelly Haider, MS, LPC**

Acknowledgments

There are so many people I want to thank for walking beside me as this book took shape.

To the women I've had the privilege to sit with in my therapy office over the years — thank you for trusting me with your stories. Your courage, vulnerability, and persistence inspired every chapter. You showed me, again and again, the extraordinary resilience women carry quietly.

To my colleagues in mental health, medicine, and research — thank you for your dedication to understanding ADHD, hormones, and the complex realities of women's lives. Your work matters, and it made much of this book possible.

To my family — thank you for your patience, your support, and your ability to love me through every stage of this journey. Even though you are grown and living your own lives, I still manage to keep you on your toes with my tangents, stories, questions, hormone storms, and "listen to this" texts. Thank you for letting me be fully myself — chaos, creativity, and all.

To my husband — thank you for loving me through every version of myself. You have stood beside me through hormone storms, emotional detours, foggy days, and moments when the ground felt like it was shifting beneath my feet. Your steadiness has been my safe place, your patience a quiet anchor, and your humor a relief when the world felt too loud. Thank you for holding me with grace through the chaos, the questions, the overwhelm, and all the unpredictable phases of this season. I am endlessly grateful to walk through it — and through life — with you.

References

Albert, K., Pruessner, J., & Newhouse, P. (2015). Estradiol levels modulate brain activity and negative emotional processing in menopausal women. Neuropsychopharmacology, 40(6), 1531–1541. https://doi.org/10.1038/npp.2015.8

American Psychiatric Association. (2022). Diagnostic and statistical manual of mental disorders (5th ed., text rev.).

Anderson, E. M., & Plante, D. T. (2023). The impact of sleep disturbances on neurocognitive functioning in adults with ADHD. Sleep Medicine Reviews, 67, 101726. https://doi.org/10.1016/j.smrv.2022.101726

Arnsten, A. F. T. (2009). The emerging neurobiology of attention-deficit/hyperactivity disorder: The key role of the prefrontal association cortex. Neuropsychopharmacology, 34(1), 2–20. https://doi.org/10.1038/npp.2008.119

Arnsten, A. F. T., & Rubia, K. (2012). Neurobiological circuits regulating attention, cognitive control, motivation, and emotion: Disruptions in neurodevelopmental psychiatric disorders. Journal of the American Academy of Child & Adolescent Psychiatry, 51(4), 356–367. https://doi.org/10.1016/j.jaac.2012.01.008

Baker, F. C., Wolfson, A. R., & Lee, K. (2018). Sleep problems during the menopausal transition: Prevalence, impact, and treatment. Nature and Science of Sleep, 10, 73–83. https://doi.org/10.2147/NSS.S158430

Barkley, R. A. (2015). Attention-deficit hyperactivity disorder: A handbook for diagnosis and treatment (4th ed.). Guilford Press.

Barkley, R. A., Fischer, M., Smallish, L., & Fletcher, K. (2002). The persistence of ADHD into adulthood: Executive function deficits and psychiatric comorbidity. Journal of Abnormal Psychology, 111(2), 279–289. https://doi.org/10.1037/0021-843X.111.2.279

Beck, A. T., & Clark, D. A. (1997). An information processing model of anxiety: Automatic and strategic processes. Behavior Research and Therapy, 35(1), 49–58. https://doi.org/10.1016/S0005-7967(96)00069-1

Bridgett, D. J., & Walker, M. E. (2006). Intellectual functioning in adults with ADHD: A meta-analytic controlled analysis. Psychological Assessment, 18(1), 12–21. https://doi.org/10.1037/1040-3590.18.1.12

Brinton, R. D. (2009). Estrogen-induced plasticity from cells to circuits: Predictions for cognitive function. Trends in Pharmacological Sciences, 30(4), 212–222. https://doi.org/10.1016/j.tips.2008.12.006

Brown, T. E. (2013). A new understanding of ADHD in children and adults: Executive function impairments. Routledge.

Buitenweg, D. C., Murre, J. M. J., & Ridderinkhof, K. R. (2012). Brain training in progress: A review of trainability in healthy seniors. Frontiers in Human Neuroscience, 6, 183. https://doi.org/10.3389/fnhum.2012.00183

Canu, W. H., & Carlson, C. L. (2007). ADHD and social adaptation in emerging adulthood. Journal of Clinical Psychology, 63(3), 234–250. https://doi.org/10.1002/jclp.20347

Castellanos, F. X., & Proal, E. (2012). Large-scale brain systems in ADHD: Beyond the prefrontal–striatal model. Trends in Cognitive Sciences, 16(1), 17–26. https://doi.org/10.1016/j.tics.2011.11.007

Cho, J. M., Lee, J., Ahn, E.-M., & Bae, J. (2025). Beyond hot flashes: The role of estrogen receptors in menopausal mental health and cognitive decline. Brain Sciences, 15(9), 1003. https://doi.org/10.3390/brainsci15091003

Conners, C. K., Epstein, J. N., March, J. S., & Angold, A. (2003). ADHD in adults: Prevalence, diagnosis, and clinical implications. Current Psychiatry Reports, 5(5), 401–408.

Cortese, S., Castellanos, F. X., Ecker, C., & Bonoldi, I. (2013). Sleep and ADHD: A systematic review. Sleep Medicine Reviews, 17(5), 349–356. https://doi.org/10.1016/j.smrv.2013.01.003

Cortese, S., et al. (2018). Practitioner review: Current best practice in the management of adverse events during ADHD pharmacotherapy. Journal of Child Psychology and Psychiatry, 59(3), 236–250.

Daley, D., & Birchwood, J. (2010). ADHD and academic performance: Why does ADHD impact on academic performance and what can be done to support ADHD children in the classroom? Child: Care, Health and Development, 36(4), 455–464.

Davidson, K. W., & Schwartz, J. E. (2020). Menopause and cognitive aging: What do we know? *Annual Review of Clinical Psychology, 16*, 239–264. https://doi.org/10.1146/annurev-clinpsy-050718-095507

De Berardis, D., Marini, S., Fornaro, M., et al. (2015). The role of estrogen in anxiety disorders. *Current Psychiatry Reports, 17*(6), 93. https://doi.org/10.1007/s11920-015-0605-y

Delaney, E., & Loughnane, M. (2021). Adult ADHD: Evidence-based treatment strategies. *Current Treatment Options in Psychiatry, 8*(3), 254–270.

Diekhof, E. K., & Gruber, O. (2010). Dopaminergic modulation of cognitive control. *Psychopharmacology, 212*(2), 243–256.

Epperson, C. N., Pittman, B., Czarkowski, K. A., & Stiklus, S. (2012). Association of estrogen with working memory during perimenopause. *The Journal of Clinical Endocrinology & Metabolism, 97*(9), 107–114.

Ernst, M., & Luciana, M. (2015). Neurodevelopmental pathways in ADHD. *Development and Psychopathology, 27*(2), 533–550.

Etkin, A., Büchel, C., & Gross, J. J. (2015). The neural bases of emotion regulation. *Nature Reviews Neuroscience, 16*(11), 693–700.

Faraone, S. V., Asherson, P., Buitelaar, J., Ramos-Quiroga, J. A., & Rohde, L. A. (2015). Attention-deficit/hyperactivity disorder. *Nature Reviews Disease Primers, 1*, 15020.

Faraone, S. V., et al. (2021). The World Federation of ADHD International Consensus Statement: 208 evidence-based conclusions about the disorder. *Neuroscience & Biobehavioral Reviews, 128*, 789–818.

Fitzgerald, P. B., & Daskalakis, Z. J. (2011). The effects of estrogen on cortical excitability. *Brain Research, 1379*, 119–127.

Greendale, G. A., et al. (2010). The menopause transition and cognition: An update. *Journal of the American Medical Association, 295*(21), 2542–2550.

Gross, J. J. (2015). Emotion regulation: Current status and future prospects. *Psychological Inquiry, 26*(1), 1–26.

Hamoda, H. M., et al. (2011). Neurocognitive function in perimenopausal women: The role of estradiol. *Menopause, 18*(5), 456–462.

Halbreich, U. (2006). Estrogen, stress, and depression. *Current Opinion in Psychiatry, 19*(6), 606–611.

Hankin, B. L., & Abramson, L. Y. (2001). Stress generation in depression. *Journal of Abnormal Psychology, 110*(3), 516–527.

Illenberger, N., & Raucher-Chene, D. (2020). The neuropsychology of adult ADHD. *Current Psychiatry Reports, 22*, 69.

Joffe, H., & Cohen, L. S. (2010). Estrogen, serotonin, and mood disturbance. *Menopause, 17*(5), 964–971.

Kessler, R. C., et al. (2006). The prevalence and correlates of adult ADHD in the United States. *American Journal of Psychiatry, 163*(4), 716–723.

Kim, A., & Baram, T. Z. (2021). Stress, corticotropin-releasing hormone, and the developing brain. *Nature Reviews Neuroscience, 22*(7), 411–425.

Leibenluft, E., & Rich, B. A. (2008). ADHD and emotion dysregulation. *Journal of Child Psychology & Psychiatry, 49*(9), 947–958.

Lenroot, R. K., & Giedd, J. N. (2010). Brain development in children and adolescents: Insights from anatomical magnetic resonance imaging. *Neuroscience & Biobehavioral Reviews, 34*(2), 213–224.

Maki, P. M. (2015). Critical window hypothesis of hormone therapy and cognition. *Current Psychiatry Reports, 17*(4), 20.

Maki, P. M., & Dumas, J. (2009). Menopause and cognitive aging: Summarizing the evidence. *Menopause, 16*(6), 1223–1231.

Marcus, D. K., & Barry, T. D. (2011). ADHD and emotion dysregulation: A meta-analysis. *Psychological Bulletin, 137*(5), 756–777.

Nigg, J. T. (2017). Annual research review: On self-regulation and executive functioning. *Journal of Child Psychology and Psychiatry, 58*(4), 361–383.

Nigg, J. T. (2022). Attention-deficit/hyperactivity disorder and executive dysfunction. *Annual Review of Clinical Psychology, 18*, 145–176.

Onn, S. P., & Grace, A. A. (2000). The role of dopamine in adult prefrontal cortex. *Progress in Neurobiology, 60*(4), 415–432.

Poon, L. W., & Rybash, J. M. (1999). The aging brain and executive function. *Aging & Mental Health, 3*(3), 224–229.

Quinn, P. O. (2005). Treating adolescent girls and women with ADHD: Gender-specific issues. *Journal of Clinical Psychology, 61*(5), 579–587.

Quinn, P., & Madhoo, M. (2014). A review of ADHD in women and girls. *The Primary Care Companion for CNS Disorders, 16*(3). https://doi.org/10.4088/PCC.13r01596

Rubinow, D. R., & Schmidt, P. J. (2019). Sex differences and the neurobiology of affective disorders. *Neuropsychopharmacology, 44*(1), 111–128.

Rubia, K. (2018). Cognitive neuroscience of ADHD. *Frontiers in Human Neuroscience, 12,* 100.

Safren, S. A., et al. (2010). Cognitive-behavioral therapy for ADHD in adults: A randomized controlled trial. *American Journal of Psychiatry, 167*(8), 950–958.

Schmidt, P. J., & Rubinow, D. R. (2016). Sex hormones and mood in the perimenopause. *Dialogues in Clinical Neuroscience, 18*(4), 385–393.

Sherwin, B. B. (2012). Estrogen and cognitive functioning in women: Lessons we have learned. *Behavioral Neuroscience, 126*(1), 123–127.

Sonuga-Barke, E. J. S. (2005). Causal models of ADHD. *Biological Psychiatry, 57*(11), 1231–1238.

Thapar, A., Cooper, M., & Rutter, M. (2017). Neurodevelopmental disorders. *Lancet Psychiatry, 4*(4), 339–346.

Thomas, R., Sanders, S., Doust, J., Beller, E., & Glasziou, P. (2015). Prevalence of ADHD in adults: Meta-analysis. *Psychological Medicine, 45*(2), 205–218.

Van der Voet, M., Harich, B., et al. (2016). Genetics of ADHD. *Psychiatric Genetics, 26*(4), 109–126.

Volkow, N. D., et al. (2009). Motivation deficit in ADHD is associated with dysfunction of the dopamine reward pathway. *Molecular Psychiatry, 14*(1), 54–66.

Volkow, N. D., Wang, G.-J., Fowler, J. S., & Telang, F. (2008). Overlapping neuronal circuits in addiction and obesity. *Philosophical Transactions of the Royal Society B, 363*(1507), 3191–3200.

Weber, M. T., Maki, P. M., & McDermott, M. P. (2014). Cognition in perimenopause: The effect of transition stage. *Menopause, 21*(11), 1173–1181.

Willett, J. B., Singer, J. D., & Martin, N. (1998). ADHD developmental trajectories. *Journal of Consulting and Clinical Psychology, 66*(3), 468–479.

Yochim, B. P., et al. (2013). Aging, executive function, and everyday cognition. *Neuropsychology, 27*(4), 474–485.

Zilverstand, A., Parvaz, M. A., & Goldstein, R. Z. (2017). Emotion regulation and the prefrontal cortex. *Neuroimage, 151*, 1–15.